MASTERING YOUR MYSTERY

HOW TO WRITE, PUBLISH, PROFIT AND PROMOTE YOUR MYSTERY

CHERYL BRADSHAW

NEW YORK TIMES BESTSELLING AUTHOR

First US edition March 2021
Copyright © 2021 by Cheryl Bradshaw
Cover Design Copyright 2021 © Indie Designz
All rights reserved.
ISBN: 9798710359617

"Always bear in mind that your own resolution to success is more important than any other thing."

—Abraham Lincoln

A Short Story About My Writing Journey

"You learn as you go, and that's
okay.
It's all a process."

In 2011, I published my first mystery novel after spending a year brushing up on the book industry, the mystery genre, and current trends in the book world. I read every self-help mystery book I could get my hands on, and I even created an organized binder for all of the notes I'd jotted down so I could reflect back on what I'd learned when needed.

I came on the scene in the golden age of indie publishing when indie writers were just starting to dip their toes into self-publishing on Amazon. Back then, it wasn't hard to get your book noticed without spending a lot of time, effort, or money. There was no need to "pay to play" like we all have to do to stay relevant now. There weren't as many authors diving into the indie pool at the rate they are now either.

When I was writing my first novel, I had no interest in publishing it as an indie book. At the time, I had a blog for aspiring authors, and many well-known mystery and thriller authors in the traditionally published world wrote guest posts offering their advice to new writers just starting out. One author I hosted was aware I had just finished writing my first book. She suggested I publish it myself instead of taking the time to get an agent. I was shocked. It was hard for me to believe a traditionally published author would suggest such a thing. She'd been around for a long time though, and she knew something I hadn't learned yet—getting your foot inside the traditionally published door is hard even when you're talented and in possession of a golden ticket. Staying inside once you're there is even harder.

I considered her advice, but I still had a "publish traditionally or bust" attitude. I created a spreadsheet where I listed every agent/agency in the mystery/thriller genres (because OCD runs rampant through my veins). After I created the list, I numbered each agency a 1, 2, or 3, depending on the agent I thought I would pair with best. For the next couple of months, I wrote various agencies hoping one of the #1 agents would be interested enough in my manuscript to work with me. I received a few positive replies, but I found the process daunting, even though I was just beginning! It ate up valuable time, and the more I thought about it, the more I realized my time would be better spent writing more books and focusing on creating my author brand.

I shelved the agent/publisher dream and developed a new strategy. My new goal was to have agents seek *me* out instead of me seeking *them* out. To achieve it, I needed to become an author worth seeking out.

I indie-published my first book for $0.99 and got to work writing the second one. Six weeks after my first book published, it entered a couple of top 100 categories on Amazon, and it remained there for several months. It was unexpected, and for the first time I thought, "Hey, maybe I *can* do this full-time one day."

From there, I created an author website, a Facebook author page, and a Twitter page, because back then Twitter was all the rage. I built up a decent following on Twitter at first, only to discover most of my core readers preferred to interact with me on Facebook. I created an author page on Facebook and then searched Facebook for indie author groups to join. I couldn't find any, and I wanted a place where indie authors could come together, so I created my own group, Indie Writers Unite. It was the first author group page on Facebook of its kind, and it's been a safe space for authors to ask questions, get advice, and learn about the book business ever since.

By 2013, I'd published three books in my Sloane Monroe series, and I was contacted by the producer of the television shows *The Glades* and *Saving Grace*. His assistant said he was interested in optioning my book series (along with a few other authors they'd contacted) for a new television show down the line. She asked me to send them information about my demographics, but I had no clue what she was talking about or how to get the information she wanted. I talked to a few author friends who had a lot more experience, and then I created and sent a portfolio that I'm sure I'd be a bit embarrassed to see now. But, hey, I did my best.

In the meantime, I put the first three books in my series into a boxed set and published it while I worked on book four. I ran a BookBub ad on the boxed set, and the following week, a good friend of mine called and asked me if I'd read the newspaper. I hadn't. She said, "You made the USA Today Best-Selling Books list." I laughed. I thought she was joking.

From the moment I hit the *USA Today* list, agents started contacting me, and for the first time, I was seeing my goals come to fruition. I talked with a few agents and signed with one of the top agents in New York City. Over the next several years, I wrote both stand-alone novels and series novels, some of which were pitched to the traditionally publishing houses, but most I published myself.

Throughout the years, I've learned a lot and I've grown a lot as a writer. I've succeeded. I've failed. I've made good decisions and bad ones. I've tried things that have worked out well, and I've tried things that didn't work at all. I've been nominated for awards, hit more bestseller lists, and I've had the chance to speak at various conferences about the book business, which is my favorite thing to do by far. I love connecting with new/upcoming writers and helping them along the way just like my fellow authors helped me. That is the reason I wrote this book.

The first half is geared toward new writers just starting out in the business, but it also includes topics and tips everyone can learn from. Wherever you are in your author journey, I wish you the best, and I hope you find it as rewarding and fulfilling as I have.

One last thing before we shove off …

I'm going to give a lot of advice and recommendations in this book. If you think they'll work for you, great! If you don't, that's okay too. When it comes to your own personal journey as an author, do what works for you, and I hope you find some nuggets of wisdom within this book that help you on your way.

—Cheryl

CONTENTS

PART
ONE:
WRITE IT

CHAPTER 1

CHOOSE YOUR WEAPON:
GENRE SELECTION

So, you want to write a mystery, thriller, or suspense novel (or you have already written one or more). How do you choose or how *did you* choose which genre and subgenre(s) to write in? Some writers think they need to stay in one lane and only publish in a single genre or subgenre. You don't need to do that, but your books do need to fit into the general scope of the genre you're writing in.

Before we dive into the current Mystery, Thriller, & Suspense categories, let's talk about category selection. I see a lot of authors promoting their books in genres that aren't even close to the type of books they've written. I just saw a thriller book with a terrorist plot in the Cozy Mystery category. Say what?! While there is some crossover from category to category—such as a mystery with a hint of romance fitting into categories like romance suspense and amateur sleuth for example—there are some categories that do not overlap.

Why do authors do it, then?

I suppose it's because they can, and also because authors want their irons in as many visibility fires as possible, thinking more visibility = more sales. That doesn't always work. Going back to the example I just used, if a fan of cozy mysteries is searching for books in the Cozy Mystery category, that reader will most likely not be interested in a book with a terrorist theme. Keep that in mind when you're choosing your categories.

If you decide to write in two very different genres, such as mystery and erotica, I'd suggest using two author names. Maybe your real name for one and a pen name for the other. Agatha Christie did this with her romance novels, which she wrote under the pen name Mary Westmacott.

Some genre categories overlap better than others. I keep the same name for my mystery series and my paranormal series because in the paranormal books there's still a murder to be solved, so some crossover exists for my fan base. On the other hand, I published a series of romance novellas years ago under my name, and at some point in the near future, I'll change the name on those books and put them under a pen name, which is what I should have done in the first place.

Moving on … Let's talk about Amazon's current category lists (as of this writing).

<u>Mystery, Thriller, & Suspense</u>

Crime Fiction
- Heist
- Kidnapping
- Murder
- Noir
- Organized Crime
- Serial Killers
- Vigilante Justice

Mystery
- Amateur Sleuth
- Black & African American
- Collections & Anthologies
- Cozy
- Hard-Boiled
- Historical
- International Mystery & Crime
- LGBT
- Police Procedurals
- Private Investigators
- Series
- Traditional Detectives
- Women Sleuths

Suspense
- Ghosts
- Horror
- Occult
- Paranormal
- Political
- Psychological

Thrillers
- Assassinations
- Conspiracies
- Crime
- Domestic
- Espionage
- Financial

- ➤ Historical
- ➤ Legal
- ➤ Medical
- ➤ Military
- ➤ Political
- ➤ Psychological
- ➤ Pulp
- ➤ Technothrillers
- ➤ Terrorism

In these four categories, there are a lot of options, but I suggest going through other fiction categories to find more options to try as well, such as Literature & Fiction and Romance to see what other subgenres might work with your book.

Mystery/Thriller/Suspense books usually fall into one of the following ten categories:

Caper

A caper is a lighthearted mystery. It's easy to read, not too intense, and witty. The protagonist could be an absentminded detective or a cat sleuth. Even though a murder is involved, the story never gets too heavy and usually has plenty of laughs throughout.

Authors to check out in this genre: Jana DeLeon, Janet Evanovich, Lily Harper Hart, Tonya Kappes, Joanne Fluke

Cozy

Cozies are similar to capers in that they are also light, fun reads. You see a lot of amateur sleuths in this genre, animal sleuths who assist in solving the crime, crimes that are culinary related (bakeries), or have to do with things like hobbies such as knitting. Sleuths might also be witches or supernatural in some way. Most often the crimes are committed in a small, tight-knit town where everyone knows each other.

Authors to check out in this genre: Shea MacLeod, Christopher Moore, Leighann Dobbs, Ann Charles, Lee Strauss, Lillian Jackson Braun

Detective/Investigator

An investigator can be a detective, a retired detective, an amateur sleuth, or a nosy neighbor. The idea behind this type of mystery is to sleuth out why the crime was committed and who committed it.

Authors to check out in this genre: Agatha Christie, Harlan Coben, Lisa Regan, Robert Dugoni, Kendra Elliot

Hardboiled

Now we're getting a lot grittier. Hardboiled novels are much more intense, detailed, and heavy. The murders are usually explained in more detail. They're more violent and sometimes graphic. The pace is fast, and the heat is constantly being turned up in these stories. This genre tends to go hand-in-hand with crime fiction, detective fiction, and even noir fiction. The protagonist has often had a hard life, has been through hell, or is still going through hell and fighting his/her inner demons.

Authors to check out in this genre: Diane Capri, Thomas Harris, Robert B. Parker, L.T. Ryan, Lee Child, Brett Battles

Noir

Noir books have a classic, dark, gritty feel to them. They often take place in an urban environment. The main character is usually a private investigator, quite often wearing a trench coat (think

Casablanca), and the characters in these books are very flawed. Lines are sometimes blurred as well, with right and wrong not always being clear.

Authors to check out in this genre: Vincent Zandri, Raymond Chandler, Caimh McDonnell, Dennis Lehane, Jo Nesbo

Paranormal/Supernatural

Paranormal and supernatural mysteries are those that combine a mystery theme while adding an element of fantasy, such as an amateur sleuth who sees/communicates with the dead, or a modern-day witch who solves mysteries using supernatural powers.

Authors to check out in this genre: Deborah Harkness, Wendy Wang, Bobbi Holmes, Darcy Coates, Willow Rose, Douglas Clegg

Police Procedural

Police procedural novels often spend more time talking about the forensics in the stories than other mystery genres do, and writers in this genre tend to do a lot more research to ensure the information they're writing about is correct (such as the difference between livor mortis, algor mortis, and rigor mortis). There's a heavy emphasis on details on everything from the crime to the forensics, autopsy, etc.

Authors to check out in this genre: Patricia Cornwell, Tess Gerritsen, Allan Leverone, Sue Grafton, Kathy Reichs, Lawrence Kelter

Suspense

Suspense books are all about keeping the reader turning pages and guessing what they think will happen in the story—whodunit, howdunit, whydunit. Many times, the protagonist will be looking to solve a problem and that problem may be in relation to the murder or be an aside to it. Readers should be holding their breath as they turn pages so the book will be near impossible to put down.

Authors to check out in this genre: M.A. Comley, J. Carson Black, Christopher Greyson, John Grisham, Liane Moriarty

Thriller

Thrillers are heavier than mysteries, and the action is consistent throughout the book. There's often a deadline in these stories, such as the protagonist having twenty-four hours to find the girl or the girl dies. Readers should feel a rush of feelings as they go through these books—from anxiety and worry to shock and surprise.

Authors to check out in this genre: Gregg Olsen, Loreth Anne White, Teresa Driscoll, Robert Dugoni, Jeffery Deaver

True Crime

True crime books are non-fiction books that deal with murders that happened in real life to real people. These are books about murder and about serial killers or those who have killed in real life.

Authors to check out in this genre: Anne Rule, Truman Capote, Vincent Bugliosi, Charles Brandt, Ronan Farrow

CHAPTER 2

THIS OR THAT: PLOTTERS AND PANTSERS

When it comes to outlining, there are two types of authors: plotters and pantsers.

Plotters are planners. They figure out their stories ahead of time and have a general knowledge of what will happen throughout the various scenes in the beginning, middle, and end. They outline in a variety of ways, including journaling, using notebooks, drawing it out with boxes and filling the boxes in, index cards, or by using PostIt Notes.

Pantsers are not planners. They may have a general idea of the main characters in the story, how the book begins, and they may even know how they think it will end, but they let the direction of the story come to them spontaneously as they write each day.

Famous Plotters: J.K. Rowling, John Grisham

Famous Pantsers: Stephen King, Margaret Atwood

I am a pantser. When I first started writing, I had every intention of plotting my books out. I even tried plotting them out.

But when I sat down to write, both the creativity and element of surprise were lacking. The words seemed disjointed and stale, which was hard for me to accept because in real life I could win a gold medal in the planner department.

I have a lot of author friends who are planners, and their books are fantastic. What doesn't work for me works for them in a big way. And they have one great advantage over me. With an outline in place, they write faster than I do.

When you're first starting out, I'd suggest trying both ways to see what feels the most comfortable. If they both feel the same, you'll get more done in the hours you spend writing as a plotter. But if you find planning to be difficult, being a pantser might be for you.

<u>You've decided to be a plotter</u>

Before I go any further on this subject, I want to recommend two amazing books to read if you're a plotter. The first is *Write Novels Fast* by Shea MacLeod and *Take Off Your Pants* (yep, you read that right) by Libbie Hawker. Shea writes faster than any author I know. I feel like a snail in comparison. The number of books she churns out each year is impressive to say the least!

Journaling or notebook plotting might take a bit longer in the beginning, but this style creates a full visual of your story. Think of it as creating a vision board of your story from beginning to end with at least the main and secondary character names, traits, and description details for your protagonist, villain, and any other main characters in your story.

Stories are divided into three parts or acts—the beginning, middle, and end, and you'll want to figure out what needs to happen in each of those acts while keeping the pacing consistent throughout each of them. For example, let's say you're aiming for a 60k word novel, you want act one to be 20k, act two to be 20k, and act three to be 20k.

While you're plotting, you'll also want to include things like:

- The title of your novel
- Ideas you have for the cover
- The location the story will take place
- The opening hook to reel in the reader
- The crime/murder (the who, what, when, where, and why)
- Red herrings (the innocent who seem guilty at first)
- Main character arc (their development from beginning to end)
- The resolution (capturing the killer/filling in any unresolved plot holes)

There's an excellent new tool for all you plotters called Plottr (of course) where you can create online storyboards, timelines, and chapters for your books. It's worth checking out.

<u>You've decided to be a pantser</u>

Well then, welcome to the exclusive, less-popular club! Like I said before, if you don't mind your novels taking a bit longer to write, this option might be perfect for you.

I've just started a new series, so I'll use it as an example of my own pantser process. The first thing I do when starting a new book is to buy a notebook for that particular book. If it has a few section dividers, that's even better. The first five or more pages are reserved for the names of every character in the book, and next to their names I list any/all relevant information. The information usually includes their name, a brief physical appearance, age, job/work information, and any quirky or important traits they might have that I might need to recall down the line. The more important the character is in the book, the more information I write about that person. Main characters might have a paragraph or more of information, whereas secondary character descriptions are briefer. As the book is being written, I continue to add to the character list as new characters arise.

Below is a list of examples from my most recent book.

MAIN CHARACTERS:

Georgiana "Gigi" Germaine (protagonist)

Detective | divorced | 42 years old | choppy, violet-colored pixie cut | dresses in vintage clothing from the 20s and 30s | has a male Samoyed named Luka | currently living in an Airstream | anger management issues | owns a 1936 Lincoln K Convertible Roadster (black, red interior) | likes to travel in her spare time | doesn't like talking about feelings | eats eggs every day | still thinks about a boy she knew in college "the one who got away"| spent the last two years off the grid because of a family tragedy

Lark Donovan

Gigi's niece | 7 years old | long blond hair | timid | afraid of the dark | has a male cat named William Shakespaw a.k.a. Willy who hides items he finds in the neighborhood in the lining of his bed | witnesses her father's murder | kidnapped by the man who killed her father

SECONDARY CHARACTERS:

Joseph "Joe" Coldwell

Phoebe's new boss | ruddy complexion, poor diet | narcissist | cheating on his wife with his new newscaster

<u>Holly Porter</u>
Phoebe's neighbor and friend | her son Ethan is Lark's best friend | always baking or cooking | Southern accent | only wears dresses and reminds Gigi of a Stepford wife

The reason I create the names and descriptions is so I have a reference I can go back to as I'm working on the book. You wouldn't believe (or maybe you would) how many times I need to make sure I have a name spelled right or get the tone of the character's personality right. When you create a character on page nine and then he/she doesn't appear again until halfway through the book, it's easy to forget the little things and make mistakes.

In the second section of my notebook, I write out the book's timeline, which I also fill in as I am writing the book. I start every book off on a Monday. It's easier for me this way. My timeline looks something like this:

DAY ONE—MONDAY—PROLOGUE

- Jack Donovan murdered
- Lark Donovan kidnapped

DAY TWO—TUESDAY—CHAPTERS 2-11 (MISSING 24 HOURS)

- Harvey visits Gigi
- Gigi returns home, resumes detective job, begins to look for Lark
- Gigi visits Joe Coldwell, Phoebe's boss

- Gigi visits the county coroner, Silas Crowe
- Gigi reminisces about Giovanni Luciana, a friend from her college years

DAY THREE—WEDNESDAY—CHAPTERS 12-16 (MISSING 48 HOURS)

- Gigi's brother's wife Tasha visits her
- Gigi receives a list from Joe of all the employees who work for the network
- Gigi gives Harvey the employee list and a thumb print recovered at the crime scene to run through AFIS
- Gigi visits Shane, Jack's office assistant, and then meets with Doctor Terry Pearson, the other doctor working in Jack's office
- Jack's office is lit on fire, Shane gets stuck inside, and he dies (poor Shane)

This timeline is one of the most important things I do because I am always referring back to it to make sure I'm getting days and times right, and if I need to fact check something I've already said, this is a quick and easy way to do it.

You'll notice I'm not very detailed in my comments, and that's because when I'm referring back, I just need to know where to look in the story for additional information. You might find adding in extra information on your own timeline is more beneficial than the overview I have here.

The third and last section in my notebook is reserved for random comments I make myself as I'm writing the book. They are reminders so I don't forget to fill in the plot holes later on. The notes say things like:

In Chapter 14, Silas tells Gigi he's recovered a viable thumb print from Lark's bedroom window. Don't forget to mention whether the print was a match to anyone from Phoebe's office or anyone in the AFIS system.

And there you have it!

Now that you have a description of plotters and pantsers, which one are you?

CHAPTER 3

> "Suspense readers are smart. They want well-written, intelligent stories, and they don't want to be duped."

What makes a good plot? Think about a few of your favorite mystery/thriller novels. What is it about those books that makes them so great? What did you like about them? Now think about a few books you didn't finish or books you stopped reading within the first few chapters. What made you put it down? For me it always comes down to one main thing: the writer failed to create a good hook.

I don't know about you, but I'm a picky reader. It takes a lot to grab my interest and hold it. I didn't used to be this way, but the longer I've been writing, the harder it is for me to go the distance with a book that fails to keep me invested page after page.

In our genre, the stakes must *always* be high, especially in the beginning. If you don't hook the reader at the start, you'll lose them.

So … how do you do that?

You start with a dramatic opening, one which grabs the reader and straps them in for the wild ride ahead.

I open most of my mysteries in third person and in the voice of the victim in the moments before they're murdered. For me, writing this way gives my readers a chance to peek through the window and witness the crime for themselves while still shielding them from who the murderer is and why the murder took place. It also does one more important thing—it makes my readers more sympathetic to the victim. By the end of the first chapter, I want readers to be fully invested. I want them to feel emotion for the victim, and I want them to care about what happened to him/her, and why.

The reason I place murder "in the first" is because I've had years to study and analyze my demographic. The audience for my main series is primarily women over the age of forty-five. They like to create an emotional attachment early on. You might have a different demographic, and we'll talk more about that a little later on.

A good rule of thumb is to start with a murder, or a scene that gives context—and a little heart-thumping—within the first few chapters. Mystery/thriller readers want to dive into the action right away. And in my opinion, it pays to give them what they want.

THE BOOK'S BEGINNING

Let's look at some examples of books that hooked me from the first page:

- A woman encounters a mysterious child on the side of the road while out jogging. (Questions: Who is the child? Why is she alone? Where are her parents?) *Find Me*, Anne Frasier

- A man is disinfecting his van's interior with bleach. (Questions: Why does he need to disinfect it with bleach? Did he just kill someone? Is he a serial killer?) *Never Look Back*, Mary Burton

- A woman leaps from her moving car. (Questions: Why do something so dangerous? Is she alone in the car? Has she been kidnapped?) *A Killer's Wife*, Victor Methos

- A man has a second to decide which way to turn. (Questions: Who is he running from? Why is he running? Is he being followed?) *The Goodbye Man*, Jeffery Deaver

- A sheriff enters a drugstore after a masked man points a gun at a pharmacist. (Questions: Who is the masked man? Why is he masked and holding a gun? What chain of events happened to cause him to do what he's doing?) *Her Broken Wings*, D.K. Hood

- A man leaves a saloon and hears the footsteps of someone following behind. (Questions: Who is following him? Why is he being followed? What does the person following him want?) *Prepper Jack*, Diane Capri

I reached out to several of my author friends and was given permission to include some of my favorite book openings that they've written in this book. As you go through these, think of the questions that come to mind after reading a single sentence.

- Mason O'hare hadn't seen the threat coming.—*Prepper Jack*, Diane Capri

- Hawk yanked on his fishing rod and started to wrestle with what he initially believed to be a fish.—*Deep Cover*, R.J. Patterson

- We're all going to die.—*Lady Rample Sits In*, Shea MacLeod

- The boys headed across the park towards the area where their parents had forbidden them to play.—*Hostile Justice*, M.A. Comley
- Thomas Edison stood on the lawn of his West Orange laboratory and watched the buildings burn.—*The Atlantis Riddle*, Kevin Tumlinson
- Dak stared through the night vision goggles at the terrorist camp on the opposite ridge.—*Out of the Fire*, Ernest Dempsey
- A stinging slap ripped Dani from unconsciousness.—*The Buried*, Brett Battles
- She's alone in the school building.—*The Extortionist*, Vincent Zandri
- Tracie Tanner shifted in her seat, fingering her gold cross necklace uncomfortably.—*The Omega Connection*, Allan Leverone
- Today she would nail the bastard.—*Hunter*, Robert Bidinotto
- Over the persistent scratch, scratch, Alexandra Carlson heard the sizzling sound of disaster.—*Night Stalker*, Carol David Luce
- Every time the bomb rattled in Dane Kanter's trunk, icy neurons fired through his bloodstream.—*A Touch of Terror*, Gary Ponzo
- It attacked with the ferocity of a wild animal.—*The Hour Before Dark*, Douglas Clegg
- I watched as my life slipped away and there was nothing I could do about it.—*Dream On*, Aaron Patterson
- I found the head.—*The List*, J.A. Konrath
- The question most people ask when they first meet me is: How does an attorney from a reputable law firm in

La Jolla end up on death row?—*Beyond Justice*, Joshua
Graham

If you haven't started writing your book yet, and you're looking
for a good idea for its plot, I'd suggest you check out Bryn
Donovan's book 5,000 Writing Prompts.

Now that you have an idea of what a good opening line looks
like, let's talk about what else should be included in those first few
chapters.

<u>You'll want to:</u>

- Start with a dramatic event
- Introduce your main character
- Reveal the crime the main character needs to solve
- Set a theme you will carry throughout the story
- Start leaving a trail of breadcrumbs for your sleuth to
  follow

It's important for your reader to realize solving the crime isn't
going to be easy. There should be multiple variables in place
sending your sleuth in different directions. This is one way to keep
your reader interested and invested in your story.

Once your reader is hooked, it's time to introduce subplots,
bring in your secondary characters, and add layers on to the main
theme. You'll also want to create speedbumps for your sleuth, things
that keep them from solving the crime too soon. The conflict you
create in the opening chapters of your book also needs to continue
developing in different ways as the story moves forward to keep
your reader anticipating what comes next.

THE BOOK'S MIDDLE

Now that your main character has been introduced, you can start adding a little more to their backstory to create a fuller picture for your readers to visualize and continue connecting with as they read on. Your main character may be smart and tough but should also have weaknesses. They may seem to be in control, only to discover they've been heading in the wrong direction the entire time. Making your main character look like they're about to succeed and then having them fail keeps the story moving and your pacing on target.

Also, don't be afraid of having your sleuth fail. Give them some failures, and then give him a win or two here and there. It's all about balance.

The middle of your mystery is where a good deal of your suspects come into play. Most will turn out to be innocent of the crime, and this is what helps your sleuth continue weeding people out until he finds the culprit he's been looking for all along.

The middle is also where your book is in the most danger of falling flat. You want to maintain the story's momentum and keep the reader turning pages. As a pantser, this is the hardest part of the book to write for me, and sometimes I have to become a plotter in this section in order to figure out how I'm going to get my reader through it while keeping it fresh and exciting.

In the middle of your book your main character faces a lot of his most difficult challenges. He's tested in multiple ways by those trying to thwart his efforts, and he is helped by those sympathetic to his need to exact justice.

Examples of what happens in the middle:

- A lot of action takes place

- The main character becomes more developed
- The main character experiences setbacks/challenges
- There's a great deal of confusion as the main character follows leads that go nowhere
- The main character is frustrated and getting more and more anxious about coming face-to-face with the villain

This is a great time to start resolving some of the smaller things and reveal some of your red herrings. If you save them all for the end, it's going to seem like you've tried to cram them all in, and that takes away from the final showdown between the sleuth and the villain. Your readers have read the entire book to get to that salacious, riveting moment, and nothing else should overshadow it. The reader deserves an ending they can focus on without other distractions.

THE BOOK'S END

By the time you get to the final chapters of your book, your sleuth should have a clear direction in which to go, including the focus to zero in on the villain and create an incredible confrontation. I like to refer to this section of the book as "the chase," because that's what's happening. The sleuth finally knows where they're going and who they're after. This is where your reader learns the truth about what happened and why. And the reader celebrates along with your sleuth as the villain is brought to sweet, sweet justice.

The end is also where the development of your main character is fully realized. Over the course of the investigation, your sleuth should have changed in some way. For example, maybe they've learned something about themselves and commit to be different in the future.

The end should button-up, tie-up, zip-up, and seal (you get the idea)—and all reader questions should be resolved without them wanting to toss their tablet or paperback book across the room after they've finished. And even though you're writing fiction, you'll lose readers if they don't find the book plausible in the end. Readers are smart. They want well-written, intelligent stories, and they don't want to be duped.

<u>Things to avoid:</u>

- Don't make the ending obvious
- Don't leave any unexplained loose ends, plot holes
- Don't make it too easy (a crime the reader can easily solve on their own)
- Don't have the villain spill his guts at the end of the story in order for the murder to be solved (it makes your reader feel ripped off)
- Don't overdo the violence and leave dead bodies all over the place when it isn't necessary
- Don't make your villain be incapable of committing the crime
- Don't end the book without the murderer being brought to justice
- Don't. Rush. The. Ending.

<u>In summary, a timeline of, say, a murder mystery happens in these steps:</u>

1. Start with an opening hook
2. Introduce and describe your sleuth

3. Murder occurs or has occurred
4. Sleuth tracks killer, faces obstacles, deals with red herrings
5. Sleuth catches killer
6. Case is resolved

CHAPTER 4

SEASON YOUR STEAK: THE POWER OF SUBPLOTS

Think of subplots as a short story within your main story. They're side stories that add to the main story without taking away from it, and the job of a subplot is to strengthen the overall story.

Not sure where to begin? It's okay. In fact, I suggest you keep the idea of adding a subplot in the back of your mind as you write your novel because your focus should always be on the main story first. As your book progresses, think of the areas that naturally lend themselves to the addition of a subplot and go from there. It shouldn't be hard work to add them. They should naturally occur when the time is right.

Let's talk about the difference between main plots and subplots.

<u>Main Plots</u>

- Always have an external conflict (a murder has occurred, and the protagonist deals with a multitude of obstacles before being able to solve it)
- Have a core relationship (which is connected to the main conflict and could involve coworkers, a romantic interest, a friend, or family members)
- Have an internal conflict (the struggle between what the protagonist thinks he should do versus what he actually does)

<u>Subplots</u>

- Use minor characters in the story who have their own personality and their own agenda
- Has characters that enter the story, play their part, and then fade out, thereby allowing the primary cast members to shine.

Why are subplots an important part of your story?

They add meat to the bone. Think of them the same way you think of your first draft and your final draft. The first draft is lean, and the final draft is what happens after you've gone back through the story and added in the necessary details that make your good story a great one.

<u>What can a well-crafted subplot do?</u>

- Add another delicious layer of meat to the story
- Add variety to the story

- Teach a moral lesson
- Provide a new plot twist
- Keep the reader invested
- Help your hero/heroine change in some way
- Reveal important information (maybe a secret)
- Add conflict between characters
- Explore the main theme in a bigger way
- Change the overall tone of the story (add heaviness or a sense of ease)
- Help move the story forward
- Change the pace (slow it down or speed it up)
- Provide an answer to a question that hasn't been answered yet
- Help manage the pacing of the story
- Create romantic tension through added suspense

Subplots can be woven into the main story (the murder investigation), or they can be separate, and one can have nothing to do with the other except for the fact that both of them relate to your protagonist in some way.

When creating a subplot figure out the goal you're trying to achieve with its creation and how it affects your main storyline.

It's important to note that unlike your main story, subplots do not need to stand on their own. They don't *need* a beginning, middle, and end. They *can* have one. They just don't always need it.

<u>Some tips for creating a subplot:</u>

- Start off with the murder, introduce the characters so the reader becomes familiar, and then start your subplot.

- Separate the subplot from the main plot by giving the subplots their own chapters. Of course, the main plot will be the bulk of your chapters since it's the main focus of the book.
- Introduce the character focus of the subplot in a place where they fit in with that particular scene (your heroine's sister, for example), and then have them not appear again for a while and then pop back into the book again when it's relevant for them to do so.
- Place a clue somewhere in the book that seems irrelevant and innocent at first but ends up becoming an important part of the mystery (Agatha Christie is an example of an author who excelled at this.)
- Write the main plot in first person and the subplot in third (James Patterson is good at this.)
- Place the subplot in one section of the book, perhaps in the middle, so it doesn't take away from the beginning or the end of the main plot.
- Use a backstory where something is revealed about a character.

When you're writing your subplots, keep in mind that you don't need too many. One or two is fine. The last thing you want to do is overwhelm the reader and stray too far from the main storyline. I'd say no more than two or three for a book in the 70k range, and up to four for books in the 100k range.

One thing I do with my subplots is to create tension between my protagonist and her love interest. As you know, when writing mysteries, we often leave sex between characters at the bedroom door and don't go into a great deal of detail. That doesn't mean there can't be tension between characters as long as it's sprinkled on and not poured. We're writing mystery, not romance. If you're writing romance suspense, you can get away with it to a degree, but just remember the hardcore mystery/thriller reader is more interested in the crime and not what's going on between the sheets.

CHAPTER 5

GOOD MEASURE: CHAPTER LENGTH

Before I discuss chapter length, I want to talk about novel lengths.

<u>Novel sizes are broken into these main categories:</u>

Flash Fiction: 100 to 7,500 words

Novelette: 7,500 to 19k words

Novella: 10k to 40k words

Novel: 50k to 100k words

Epic Novel: Over 110k words

You could line up a group of authors and ask how long each one thinks a chapter should be, and you'd receive a variety of answers. The truth is there's no one size fits all when it comes to chapter length. I've heard some people say every chapter they write is four pages long. Other writers say ten. Others say the chapter ends when it needs to end. The choice is up to you.

Readers today are not the readers of yesterday. Most readers today lead busy lives. They don't have as much time as they used to, so fast-paced mysteries suit them well. These types of readers know that when they pick up a book, they'll be lucky to get through a chapter or two before they need to set it down. Retirees tend to have a lot more time on their hands, and for them, it may not matter if a chapter is ten pages long. Younger readers have a lot more going on and not as much time to devote to reading all of the time.

When thinking about your own chapter length, a few of the biggest things to consider is your own reading demographic:

- Are they primarily male or female?
- Or are they a mix of male and female?
- What age group buys your books the most?

If you're a new writer just starting out, you won't know this yet, but as you publish more and more books, you'll be able to gather valuable data to let you know who your readers are, and this data will help you write books that cater to your core audience.

"More than anything, your focus should always be on furthering the momentum of your story."

I have read in several places that the average number of words in a chapter is 4,000. I personally don't go into a chapter thinking I need to get it to an X number of pages or words. I think of chapters in terms of a beginning, middle, and end. Let's say my sleuth goes to a house to question a suspect. The beginning is going to the house, the middle is questioning, and the end is either leaving the house or being led in a whole new direction. Some suspects need to be questioned more than others. I don't like to add filler just for the sake of adding it. It causes readers to start skipping sections of your book—something you must avoid.

I'd say the majority of my chapters are around four or five pages long. But I have also written chapters that are one page, and several that are even less than one page. Instead of focusing on where they end, I focus on the cliffhanger. It's more important to me to end as many of my chapters as I can with a sentence that keeps the reader reading even when it's way past their bedtime. Your focus should always be on furthering the momentum of your story. And as you transition from one chapter to the next, make those transitions as smooth as possible.

When planning the end of your chapters, make sure the reader leaves off in a place where they'll look forward to picking the book back up again instead of becoming bored, forgetting about it, and moving on to a different book. I wouldn't worry too much about this when writing your first draft. When you read through the book in its entirety during the editing process, you'll get a good idea of the overall tone and pace, what works, and what feels disjointed and out of place.

Even though I don't follow specific rules with my chapters, there are a few reasons why it's sometimes better to keep their lengths fairly consistent.

1. Chapters that are too long can become too much for your reader to digest, especially if there are too many

changes within a single chapter that could have been broken up into two or three smaller chapters.

2. When the chapters are the same, the pacing of your book tends to be the same, and there's a nice ebb and flow to it.

CHAPTER 6

WHAT THE %*&#@!
CURSING IN FICTION

The wording you choose to use in your novels is up to you. It's your book, and it's your characters. That said, does foul language matter? It does. And depending on your fan demographic, it might matter a little or it might matter a lot.

I used the "F" word in the first book I ever wrote. I was writing a scene where my protagonist was physically attacked by a real piece of crap who had her pinned against a wall. The scene was heavy and intense. The "F" word was the only word suited to the situation, and I used it.

Since then, I can count on one hand the number of times I've used that particular word again. The reason I don't swear often in my books is because:

1. I don't personally feel it's needed in order to write a good story in the mystery genre, though thriller writers can get away with it a bit more.

2. My target audience often mentions how "clean" my books are in their reviews. I've received too many reviews like this to ignore it—it's clearly an important snippet of data relating to my overall reader demographic.

In real life, I swear—more like a sailor's daughter than a sailor, but my target audience needn't be privy to that. All they need to know is what's on the pages I write. I have no problem using swear words in my books, but I generally stick to words like "hell" or "damn." To date, I have never used the words "God," or "Christ," and that's because everyone has a differing opinion of spirituality and religion, and I've decided not to "poke the religious bear," so to speak.

Let's go back to the first book I wrote for a moment. One woman reviewed it and said, *"I do not understand why she had to use f—so much."*

Keep in mind, the word was used ONCE in the entire book. One flipping time! Get over it, lady!

Figure out your core demographic as soon as you can. If it's primarily women over fifty, consider using less swear words. If it's a younger demographic, consisting of women and men, you'll be able to get away with it more.

Just yesterday I received an email from a reader, and this is typical of the kind of emails I receive:

"I am reading the Sloane Monroe series, and I am currently reading Bed of Bones. I truly enjoy reading your books, and I really appreciate the fact that there are no sex scenes or swearing in the books. It is truly refreshing."

But what do other readers think? I polled mine, and here's what they had to say:

"I think swearing is acceptable. The amount of swearing depends on the character. For instance, a mother of young children who is dealing with an intense and stressful moment would swear, but it would be minimal, and in that moment only. A low level, petty criminal on the other hand could swear up a storm and that's definitely acceptable."—Amanda K.

"If it is part of the story and fitting to the character, then yes. If it's being used because the author couldn't think of other words to use, then no."—Nancy N.

"I think it's okay to have a little swear words with the right character. Just don't go overboard and use God's name in vain."—Linda P.

"I don't mind a little bit, but too much ruins the plot and makes me give up on the book."—Belinda M.

"I very deliberately avoid books with intense cursing in them. There are so many other words in the English language to choose from. Why lower yourself to cursing? It offends me."—Sally W.

"I don't mind a little bit of swearing if it fits the character's personality. I can't stand it if it's every other word that comes out of their mouth. That's a big turn off for me in books."—Julie L.

"Words like 'shit' or 'damn' or 'hell' don't bother me. Taking the Lord's name in vain turns me off, however!—Barbara W.

"Swearing if it suits the situation is okay, as there are people who

swear all the time. You can swear without using the 'C' and 'F' words, which are unnecessary and lowers the grade of the author's writing."—Rosalynd B

"I would prefer no 'F' bombs and no use of the word 'God.' Any other swear word is acceptable in the proper context."—Barb H.

"Some swearing is fine. The constant use of the F-word doesn't enhance the story, and usually it's a distraction. There are plenty of words to describe a situation, a person, or a feeling. But there are times when an expletive is all that fits (shock, pain, etc.)"—Mickey N.

"I do not mind at all if authors have their characters swear. In fact, there are some instances where a good swear word is the only thing to say."—Dorothy B.

*"I don't mind the occasional curse word, but I get put off if a book is riddled with bad language. Some words are very off putting too (c**t is particularly obnoxious to me). It feels more acceptable to me if the word used fits with the character's persona too."*—Tanya N.

"I think it depends on the context. I hate reading books where men use foul language to describe women, especially during sex. I also hate the C word. If the swear words are part of the character's personality, it makes sense, but seeing the F word five or six times on one page makes me feel like the author is unimaginative."—Patty L.

"The only thing that bothers me is the F word and using God's name in vain. I know bad language is part of life. It is just those two that really bother me."—Jackie R.

"Swearing doesn't bother me unless it serves no purpose. Dropping F-bombs all the time is unnecessary. I lose respect for the author who

uses swearing to replace conversational dialogue. Communication is key to relationships and swearing is not communication."—Caryn H.

"I just ignore them and move on!"—Uma R.

I received a lot more comments than the ones you've just read, but these were what the majority of my readers had to say. From this I'd suggest swearing is acceptable to most as long as a book isn't riddled with it and when a few of the harsher swear words are used sparingly.

CHAPTER 7

GO AHEAD, PUSH ME: WRITING GREAT CLIFFHANGERS

We all have things we like doing more than others in our writing. For me, cliffhangers are among my favorite things to write. There's nothing more satisfying than receiving messages and reviews from readers who say they were only going to read one or two chapters but then they ended up staying up all night to finish the entire book. This is why we write stories—to keep the reader turning pages.

<u>What is a cliffhanger?</u>

It's a sudden change or plot twist that leaves the readers hanging because it hasn't been resolved. In short, it's prolonged suspense.

Cliffhangers at the end of a chapter generally happen because one of two things have occurred:

1. An important, shocking revelation has bubbled to the surface.
2. The protagonist has stumbled upon an immediate threat.

Readers like to be shocked when they're reading a story. Cliffhangers pave the way for that to occur, and they keep the story from being too predictable. They give your readers an exciting, fun challenge to keep on going even when they're tired and want to stop.

Including cliffhangers at the end of chapters is a great way to engage the reader ... as long as there is a quick resolve at the beginning of the next chapter. It's important to note, however, that you probably should avoid ending the book with a cliffhanger, even if the book is part of a series. Readers in our genre do not look favorably on a book that doesn't give them closure in the end. Writers of other genres can get away with it. We can't.

Some authors think they can't end a chapter with a cliffhanger if the scene they're working on isn't finished, but you can. Just make sure there's some form of resolve in the chapter that follows it.

> "When a reader finishes a chapter,
> he makes a decision about whether
> to put the book down or keep on going.
> If you craft a brilliant cliffhanger, the
> decision
> will have already been made for
> them."

<u>When writing a powerful cliffhanger:</u>

- Make it abrupt. If it's lengthy and drawn out it won't have the same impact.

- Start the next chapter diving into what has occurred, and don't draw it out for too long. Address it and move on. However, don't be afraid to keep turning up the heat and making the situation even more perilous than it already is.

- Change your cliffhangers up. Don't use the same type all the time. For example, if one cliffhanger ends with an interesting tidbit of dialogue, end the next one with a question.

<u>Ideas for good cliffhangers:</u>

- End the chapter with a question
- Reveal something that catches the reader off-guard (element of surprise)
- Have the last line end with dialogue
- Create a high or low point for the protagonist/main character
- Put the protagonist in harm's way (hit over the head, knocked unconscious, in a house that's on fire, realizes she's being followed, etc.)
- Reveal unexpected information
- Convey emotion, a thought or comment that connects with the reader in some profound way, such as having the protagonist experience a loss/setback
- Have the protagonist close to solving the crime, but at the last second an unforeseen twist throws them off

- Reveal something exciting is about to happen
- Create urgency (time is running out)
- A serious decision needs to be made
- Make it seem like something will happen but then it doesn't (gun aimed but not fired, a character thinks they're about to be kissed, and it doesn't happen, etc.)
- Give a hint about what's coming next but don't give details (drop breadcrumbs from one chapter to the next)
- Hit one of the characters with a shocking accusation

It's important to note your cliffhangers should blend in well with the story, connect at the right time, and not come out of nowhere. In other words, they need to be plausible and realistic enough for the reader to believe.

Here are some examples of cliffhangers from my book *Gone Daddy Gone*:

1. *Sleep tight, everyone. I'll be coming for you all soon.*

In this example, the reader is inside the mind of the killer as he peers through a window, watching my protagonist sleep. She has no idea he's there, stalking her.

2. *She was a professional escort.*

At first this doesn't seem like much, but the reader has just received a shocking revelation. The squeaky-clean college girl has been moonlighting on the side as an escort. It pushes the reader to ask all kinds of questions like:

- How did she become an escort?
- How long has she been an escort?
- What services did she offer as an escort?
- Why would a seemingly innocent girl get into the escort business?

3.   *"I'll explain everything when you get here."*

This is the perfect example of ending a scene before it is finished. There are unanswered questions that need to be resolved, and the reader must keep going in order to find out what is explained.

4.   *I didn't call Coop, and I hoped it wasn't a mistake.*

The protagonist is questioning herself here. She made a rash decision and now that it's been made, she's worried about the potential fallout if the decision she made was wrong.

5.   *Inside the room was Elise, face down in a pool of blood, and Paul sitting in front of her, waving the gun above his head, laughing.*

There's a lot to unpack here, starting with what we assume to be a dead woman and an unstable man who seems to have shot her.

6.   *He had only felt real love for a woman once, and that woman had been his wife. When he lost her, he lost everything.*

This implies a certain amount of desperation on the man's part. He's lost *everything*. A desperate person with nothing more to lose is a ticking time bomb set to go off.

7. *There was a different path I needed to follow, perhaps one much closer to home, and I just needed to find it.*

The protagonist is taking a turn now. She's left the path she's been on and has started down a new one. As the writer, I know what it is, but I don't divulge yet. The reader must keep reading if they want to find out.

8. *I fell to his side, hovering over him, screaming.*

The protagonist's fiancé has just been shot. I cut the scene here without saying whether he's dead or alive. It's brutal to the reader, I know. But it holds their interest, and that's what I'm after.

9. *"That's right, Sloane. Follow me. Take the bait."*

We're back inside the killer's mind here. He's just set a trap for Sloane, and the reader is left to wonder not only what will happen next, but what the killer will do if he captures her.

10. *Attached to the fabric was a playing card, this time the Jack of Hearts. Written on the card was a message: How does it feel to lose the one you love?*

Here, my protagonist realizes the killer's motive is personal. She now understands he's going after the people she loves and picking them off, until she's the only one left. This shifts the direction of the story yet again.

11. *I just shook my head because I didn't dare say what I was thinking—not until I was sure.*

The protagonist believes she's worked out the identity of the killer. The reader will need to continue on if they want to know what she's thinking and whom she suspects.

> *12. Shelby was dead because of me. Cade was fighting for his life because of me. And now Gran. I only hoped we found her before … I couldn't allow myself to think it.*

The protagonist has been through hell by this point. In a last attempt to bend her to his will, the killer abducts her grandmother, and the chase is on to see if she finds her in time.

> *13. He didn't blame her, and he hated to admit he'd enjoyed her company. It was almost a shame she had to die.*

The protagonist has been captured by the killer, and her fate is in his hands … or is it? ;)

> *14. Before I could stop him, he aimed the gun at Gran and fired.*

Here again, the reader is filled with questions. She has no idea if the bullet hit Gran or missed her or if Gran is alive or dead. In order to find out … yep, you guessed it. The reader must continue on to the next chapter.

CHAPTER 8

LOCATION, LOCATION, LOCATION: CREATING THE PERFECT AMBIANCE

I once did a Q & A session with a couple hundred of my avid readers in a private Facebook group, and I allowed them to ask me anything they wanted. Thankfully, they weren't too hard on me! I was surprised to learn several of them wanted to know if I had been to the locations my books are set in.

The answer is no, I haven't. I have been to the majority of them, and for the few I haven't visited, a lot of research went into getting an accurate feel for those locations. There's nothing like a reader getting excited about your book because it's based in their hometown or a place they love to visit, only to have them discover a lot of discrepancies in the setting, which, in turn, sours the experience for them.

Whether I've been to the town/city or I haven't, I love researching unique settings for my books, and I like writing about places near and dear to my heart.

"Think of a setting as if it were an extra character, because in many ways, it is just that."

If I asked you to close your eyes and visualize your happy place, where are you? On the beach? In the mountains? At your grandfather's house?

Settings offer readers a rich experience. For a short time, the setting sweeps them up and welcomes them along for the journey, even though in reality they might be curled up in front of the fire in the privacy of their own home.

Just yesterday I was writing a scene where the kidnapper requested the ransom money for the female hostage he was keeping to be taken to the park at midnight. The setting was fine. There's nothing wrong with meeting up at a park.

I started thinking about the setting of the book itself, which is New Orleans. And I realized a park wouldn't do New Orleans justice if I didn't add more flavor to a unique city that's unlike any others I've been to before. Why choose to have the ransom money taken to the park when it could be taken to one of the most haunted places in New Orleans … Cemetery No. 1? Mwahaha. With a few tweaks, I made the change, and the story was enriched because of it.

When you sit down to create your main cast of primary and secondary characters, you should also decide where the book will take place. Some writers choose to keep every book in their series in the same city or town. Depending on the city, a series could go on forever with endless possibilities of creative ways to make the most of the place.

Other writers prefer to branch out and take their protagonist on the road. One thing I loved about Agatha Christie's novels was that she moved Poirot around, sticking him into settings which suited her based on some of the experiences she'd had in her own life. Her novel *Murder on the Orient Express* combined her affection for the Orient Express—which she traveled on in 1928—with the inspiration for the plot—the abduction of Charles Lindbergh's baby, which was in newspaper headlines at the time. It's a superb example of a setting becoming its own character in a mystery. Likewise, Christie's novel Death on the Nile, set in Egypt, is another great example of how she used an exotic place she'd visited as the backdrop for one of her most famous novels of all time.

Once you know where your book will be set, it's time to get to know the location well. If you've never visited, one easy thing you can do is to Google something like this: top twenty attractions in New Orleans.

I tend to look on Tripadviser for this because they list out the most popular attractions in order, starting with the most popular.

From there, I look at a lot of photos of the place, and if I'm setting a specific scene somewhere that isn't fictional, I want to make sure the description and the timeline/time of year is accurate. For example, at the beginning of my book set in New Orleans, the victim's band is playing at the Crescent City Blues & Barbecue Festival. This is a real festival that takes place every year in October, which means it's the time of year the book needs to be set in as well, and it was up to me to make sure everything reflected that.

Here's an example of a basic outline I used based on the scenes I created:

<u>Location: New Orleans, Louisiana</u>

Time of Year: fall, mid-October
Weather: 65-75 degrees
Colors: Burnt orange, yellow, red on the trees, blue skies.

Sights: Eerie darkness of Cemetery No. 1 at night, leaves on the ground, rain, fall festivals.

Smells: On warmer days, downtown French Quarter still smells like piss in a frying pan but is often masked by the aroma of creole cooking—jambalaya, gumbo, red beans and rice, shrimp boil, bananas Foster, muffaletta. The aroma of fragrant flowers fills the streets of some neighborhoods as well.

Sounds: Jazz music drifting through the pubs and bistros on Frenchmen Street.

Clothing: Long sleeves and lightweight jacket for evening, T-shirt during the day.

Concerns: Hurricane season, possible storms and flooding.

Tastes: Po' boy from Parkway Bakery, Oysters Rockefeller at Antione's, Beignets from Café DuMonde.

One final word of caution before I exit this chapter. Be careful when using real settings, especially if you say something negative/derogatory. For example, it's not a good idea to write a scene using a famous fast-food chain and then to say the food was horrible. I'm not saying you'll get sued, but why take that chance?!

CHAPTER 9

WHAT A CHARACTER: PROTAGONISTS AND MAIN CHARACTERS

I love creating characters and adding in little oddities to make them interesting and unique. Main characters should be relatable to your readers, someone they can connect with on a personal level. Whether prickly or tenderhearted, the main character is the glue that holds the story together, and you want these characters to be compelling enough to keep the reader turning pages.

What's important when it comes to creating a memorable character?

A memorable character is someone who is real enough to be believable and not a clichéd, cardboard cutout. Readers like to put themselves into the character's shoes and to laugh and cry with them as if they were real, because through the eyes of your reader, in a way, they are.

> "Character is like a tree and
> reputation like a shadow.
> The shadow is what we think of it;
> the tree is the real thing.
> —Abraham Lincoln"

Protagonists vs. Main Characters

What is the difference between a main character and a protagonist?

Protagonists are the center of the story, the number-one person the story revolves around.

Main characters are those who have important, prominent roles in the story, but serve second in command to the protagonist (think of them in terms of president and vice president).

Protagonist/Main Character Examples:

Harry Potter and Ron Weasley
Tony Stark and Pepper Potts
Star-Lord and Rocket Raccoon
Indiana Jones and Marion Ravenwood
Mulan and Commander Tung
Elle Woods and Emmett

In novels of mystery/thriller/suspense, there are usually protagonists, main characters, and secondary characters. But not always. The bestselling book *Big Little Lies* by Liane Moriarty is a great example of a mystery where several characters all play the lead role. Madeline, Celeste, Jane, Renata, and Bonnie all have major roles in the book, passing the baton from one to the other as the scenes shift.

Once you have your protagonist and main characters worked out, it's time to figure out what makes them tick.

<u>In creating your protagonist and main characters, here are some questions to help flesh them out:</u>

- Who are they?
- What makes them tick?
- What are their interests?
- What are their likes/dislikes?
- How were they raised and where?
- What's their personality like? (introvert/extrovert, witty, cunning, sassy, etc.)
- How do they talk? (accent or no accent, good grammar/ poor grammar, etc.)
- Why are they who they are right now, and how did they get where they are now?
- Are they a glass-half-full type, or half-empty kind of person? Why?
- What pushes them to their breaking point?
- When life is hard, where do they find comfort? (person, place, etc.)
- How can you make who they are today grow into someone better tomorrow?
- Who are their friends?
- Who are their enemies?
- Who is their family?
- How many brothers and sisters?
- Where did they go to school? Did they go to college? What did they study?
- Are they single? Dating? Married?

- What are their fears?
- What makes them feel embarrassed?
- Does he/she have secrets? What would happen if those secrets came out?

Some of this information isn't necessary for main characters, but they should be considered for your protagonist. Your protagonist needs to be a strong, solid character because the journey they're about to take won't always be easy, and no matter how hard it gets or how many times they stumble and fall, they need to be able to push through to the bitter end.

With that said, let's go over a few of the most beloved characters of all time and the reasons readers fell in love with them.

Elizabeth Bennet (Pride and Prejudice)
If I had lived in another era, I believe I could have actually been Lizzie Bennet. Her brazen, feisty personality and flare for life is exciting and memorable. Readers keep turning pages because she's unpredictable, and they can't wait to see what she will say or do next. She speaks her mind, and she's respected for it. She thinks highly of herself, even though there are those in positions much higher and wealthier than she is in her station, and readers love that part of her.

Nancy Drew (Nancy Drew Mysteries)
Nancy Drew is smart, analytical, and almost always keeps her cool, even when she's under pressure. She's popular. People like her, and people listen to her. She has determination and drive, and she's not afraid to take risks, even when it means she puts herself in harm's way. Readers expect her to get into sticky predicaments, and they read with interest to find out what obstacles she's about to overcome.

Hercule Poirot (Agatha Christie Mysteries)

When I think of Hercule Poirot, I think of the game Clue. Poirot is the perfect example of what readers are looking for in a good mystery—the chance to tag along with him and see if they can solve the crime before he does. Poirot gives his utmost attention to even the smallest detail. He rarely gets things wrong, and his proud, snobby, and charming demeanor makes him a character that readers have clamored about for decades.

Interesting side note … while readers share a fondness for him, Agatha Christie grew tired of him over time, and by 1960, she was ready to kill him off for good. She didn't though. Why not? Because she knew it would be unfair to her readers who blew through her books and kept asking for more Poirot novels.

Hannibal Lecter *(Silence of the Lambs)*

He may not be the sanest person you'll ever meet. And sure, he chowed down on a man's liver with a side of fava beans and a refreshing glass of chianti. And yet, after we'd learned these gruesome details about him and what made him tick, most of us rooted for him anyway.

Why do you think that is?

What redeemable qualities does Hannibal have that make us see him as someone other than a monster, someone we decide to give a free pass?

Why do we like him?

Hannibal makes a reader question themselves. He gets right in their face. He says, "This is who I am," and he offers no apologies. He makes us uncomfortable, but we keep on reading because he brings out a sympathetic side we never thought we could feel for a character like him. Hannibal is the perfect example of writing a character who evokes emotion, gets into our head, and changes our perception.

Throughout *Silence of the Lambs* and the subsequent books, Hannibal has multiple opportunities to harm Clarice. He doesn't, which makes us feel okay not to despise him. We convince ourselves he has redeemable qualities, which means he's not *all* bad. Right?

Jane Eyre

Jane Eyre is an example of a compelling, haunting character who isn't like any of the other characters I've mentioned so far. She's quiet, timid, seen by others as plain and ordinary, and has been treated poorly most of her life. As her backstory is revealed, we feel sorry for her, and we hope she'll finally find the happiness she's always deserved. When she doesn't, we are devastated and left wishing things could have worked out differently.

Veruca Salt *(Charlie and the Chocolate Factory)*

Veruca Salt is the kind of character you want as a secondary character or a character with a small role, but not as a main. Why? For starters, she's a brat. She's the kind of character a reader can't root for because we can't find any redeeming qualities to convince us she's worth our sticking around. When she exits the story as a "bad egg," we're thrilled to see her go.

Dorian Gray *(The Picture of Dorian Gray)*

For those of you who write supernatural suspense, Dorian Gray is an excellent example of an interesting character. When a portrait of him is painted by Hallward, Dorian becomes obsessed with staying the way he is in the painting, even if it means bartering his own soul away. I love his character because he's an example of someone you love one moment and hate the next. Think about a TV series you've seen where you started off liking the character and thinking he could do no wrong, but one season later your perspective has changed and now you loathe him. This isn't easy to create in a character, but it's very powerful when you do. Another example of this kind of character would be Ebenezer Scrooge.

Jack Reacher *(Killing Floor)*

I wanted to end this list with someone relevant to our time. A former major in the US Army Military Police Corps, Reacher is a tall, badass, independent contractor who travels the country and always manages to get involved in suspicious, dangerous situations. He doesn't own a driver's license, doesn't pay taxes, doesn't answer to anyone, and always seems to be one step ahead of anyone tracking him. He's the perfect example of a "tough guy," which is why he's adored by men and women alike.

The examples I've just listed are some of the best literary characters in history. And even though they're all different from each other, these characters have certain things in common.

Strong characters have the following:

- A storyline with a compelling motive
- Purpose and desire (a reason for doing what they do)
- Doubts (things don't always go their way)
- Fears (spiders, a former stalker they had finding them again, dying, etc.)
- Quirks (ways they stand out from everyone else)
- Character flaws, imperfections, and vulnerabilities
- Strong, rich personalities
- Love (this could be a pet, partner, family member, friend, old flame)
- Personalities that your readers relate to in some way
- Pain and suffering as part of their growth
- Opinions and specific ways they think about things
- Heroic qualities

Drawing from your own experiences:

People who know me personally always assume my protagonists are based on me and my personality. They're right and wrong. At the moment, I have three main series. All of my protagonists are women (so far), and although none of them are the same, they all capture a small part of me in different ways.

It's fine to draw on your own experience as a base and a starting point, but then you should expand the character so he/she becomes their own entity. Some of my main characters are based on a quirk or oddity of someone I've come across in my life, but none of them are an exact replica of anyone—not even me.

This might be a good spot for me to mention what I write at the start of all of my books as a disclaimer (and I'd advise you never to publish a book without saying something to this effect, just to be on the safe side):

This book is a work of fiction. Names, characters, places, businesses, and incidents either are the products of the author's imagination or are used in a fictitious manner. Any similarity to events or locales or persons, living or dead, is entirely coincidental.

CHAPTER 10

Ding, Dong, Dead:
The Victim

Before the murder and before the investigation, there's a victim. What kind of victim keeps a reader interested? I'd say it depends on the demographic of people who read your book. Mine appear conservative on the outside with splashes of bad boy/girl on the inside. I once tried to write a mafia boss out of a series. When my readers caught on, I received a lot of emails telling me how much they adored him, and they asked me to keep him alive in the books in one form or another. I actually love his character. I only considered writing him out because once I tested my demographic, I thought he might have been too aggressive for them. Turns out, I was wrong.

Sometimes we make decisions based on things we believe to be true, and we end up being wrong. As writers, we're always going to make mistakes here and there, but mistakes give us the opportunity to learn and grow. In my case, I listened to what my readers had to say, and their beloved mafia boss is alive and well today. I've just moved him to a different series.

In part two of this book, we'll dive into demographics a bit more and how they relate to the books you write. For now, let's get back to the question about what keeps a reader invested. Above all, I believe it's the emotional connection to your sleuth and to your victim.

When I wrote my first book, *Black Diamond Death*, the victim in the story goes skiing one morning, crashes on a black diamond ski run, and dies. Soon after, my protagonist, a private investigator named Sloane Monroe, is hired by the victim's sister, and Sloane discovers the victim was poisoned. At this point, the investigation begins.

Looking back now, I'd say there were things I did right with book one in the series and things I did wrong.

<u>What I did right</u>

1. I created an interesting protagonist for Sloane. My readers have followed the series for over a decade.
2. I started the book out in third person from the POV (point of view) of the victim. This reeled readers in and made them care about the victim and why she was murdered, and it also set the tone for me to continue doing this in all of my future books.

<u>What I did wrong</u>

1. The victim was compelling, but not compelling enough, in my opinion, and that's why I revised the book last year. The story is the same. I just did what I could to improve on it. I won't ever be completely happy with it, but I do recognize the beauty that's found in a first creation. It acts as a springboard from which you can learn from and become better.

2. I should have made the first book in the series a lot more personal to my protagonist. How? By making the victim someone Sloane (the private eye) knew personally. For example, Sloane's sister could have been murdered, or her niece could have been kidnapped, etc. Why? Because now I know my demographic invests the most in these kinds of stories. And once you publish a few books, you'll start to learn about your own demographic and what makes them tick.

<u>The victims in your stories (the well-liked ones) should</u>:

- Be worth saving
- Have a sense of humanity
- Evoke sympathy
- Be honored and respected
- Have a few enemies (even though they're good people)

I tend to write about victims who are decent people overall. My demographic prefers this type of victim, so that's why I don't stray too far from it. But not all writers want a victim who is squeaky clean, and not all readers want that either. You might find your demographic is much different than mine.

When writing victims who aren't as highly regarded, you have a few options. The two most prominent would be to have the victim be someone everyone despises, but maybe that victim ends up having some redeemable quality, or to have the victim appear to be a sweet, innocent type at first glance, and throughout the story (well after the reader is hooked), it's revealed they were actually a despicable person in real life and had a gift for hiding it from everyone.

When the victim is despised, you can lure the reader in by making them feel something for the family members whom the victim left behind, those who struggle the most with the victim's death. By shifting the compassion from the victim to his family, the reader remains satisfied because they still have someone to care about.

While we're on the subject of victims, let's go over the main reasons they become victims in the first place.

<u>Why do people get murdered? Here are several probable scenarios</u>:

- Anger: the victim offended the wrong person
- Jilted love: the victim was involved in a love triangle
- Accident: the victim was in the wrong place, wrong time (his car breaks down, he knocks on the door of a house nearby, is thought to be an intruder, and is shot)
- Money: the victim inherits a lot of money and is killed either by someone trying to steal it for themselves or by a family member who is filled with jealous rage because she thought the money would be left to her
- Lust: they are the object of someone's obsession
- Secrets: the victim stumbled upon something they shouldn't have (witnessed money being stolen, saw the boss engaged in inappropriate behavior with employee)
- Jealousy: the victim received a promotion over someone else

CHAPTER 11

BAD BOYS (AND GIRLS): CREATING THE PERFECT VILLAIN

I can't tell you how many times people have said, "It must be hard for you to write about the bad boy (or girl)." It's not hard at all. I love it, which sometimes confuses people. Over the years, I've learned some people don't understand how we authors are even capable of writing villains. We all have our own methods of diving into madness. Mine comes from an aberrant interest in forensics and a curiosity to know why people do the things they do. What about you?

Before I dive in further, I want to recommend a great book on this subject called Bullies, *Bastards, and Bitches: How To Write The Bad Guys Of Fiction* by Jessica Morrell. It's a great place to start if you haven't had much experience writing about bad boys (and girls).

<u>Let's talk serial killers:</u>

"Serial killers don't have to be the most evil people on the planet."

The books I write where the villain is a serial killer are some of the deepest, richest books I've written because I like to give the serial killer his own chapters and allow the reader to dive deeper into his backstory so they can get a good idea of what goes on in his/her mind and why.

Your serial killer doesn't need to be a cliché to be menacing and believable. In other words, serial killers don't have to be the evilest people on the planet. They deserve to be layered in a similar way to your protagonist because they are generally a big part of your story.

<u>What do we know about serial killers—not the fictitious ones, but the real ones?</u>

They've been studied for years, and these studies have shown interesting similarities and patterns.

A serial killer by definition is a person who commits more than three murders in a short time span or someone who commits multiple murders and spaces them out. For example, the killer might murder a number of people over a certain period of time, have a cooling-off period where they go into hiding, and then rise up to kill again.

<u>As children and teenagers, many notable serial killers in history:</u>

- Had controlling parents (especially a dominating mother)
- Had a mother/father who was abusive in some way

(physically, mentally, or both)

- May have been given up for adoption (which fed into their feelings of abandonment in some cases)
- Wet the bed for years
- Felt lonely and isolated
- Didn't fit in with others in school or in their community
- Have a form of brain damage
- Were daydreamers/fantasizers
- Experienced some kind of childhood trauma
- Started out with minor crimes like arson, the destruction of property, theft
- Lacked the bonding/affection/touch needed between infant/parent(s)
- Raised in a home with a single parent, usually their mother, after their father walked out or a divorce happened
- Were rebellious in some way
- Learned to be good liars
- Had nightmares
- Lacked sympathy or empathy and seemed incapable of feeling guilty about the things they'd done
- Developed rage because of a lack of bonding
- Were psychopaths

Serial killers as adults:

- Think of themselves in a Godlike way, maybe even fantasizing they are a God in their own right—because when they kill and get away with it, they feel powerful. They may even fantasize they are God.

- Are controlling and dominant, just as they were controlled and dominated when they were young
- Can appear to be perfectly normal in their everyday life—some are even married and have a family of their own, and the family often has no idea this person is living a double life.
- Usually target women or children, particularly if they are heterosexual, although I *strongly* advise leaving children out of the equation in this scenario unless you're writing a darker type of thriller (see my chapter on pets/kids)
- Test out the waters with their first kill, which may be and often times is quite sloppy, and once they get away with it, they refine it and become better over time
- Become addicted to the act of killing, as a drug user becomes addicted to some drugs. They just want more. When they get away with it once, they want to do it again and again
- Like to relive their crimes, so they'll take "trophies" from each victim and/or they return to the scene of the crime
- Often times three or more murders take place in a two-week period

<u>Many serial killers are either organized or become more organized as they go, which means they:</u>

o   Prefer to choose a stranger over someone they know
o   Stalk their victims and get to know their routine
o   Have a rational conversation with the victim when meeting them

o   Have what they need to carry out initial kidnapping (weapons, restraints)

o   Have a plan (where they'll grab the victim, where they'll take them, how they will dispose of them)

o   Control victims with threats, lies, and manipulation

o   Ensure the crime takes place far from their own residence

o   Become better at killing over time

o   Are aware of police procedures, including investigations/ forensics

o   Track the investigation as it occurs to learn how it's being handled which benefits them for the next time they decide to kill

<u>Types of serial killers</u>

Hedonistic

This type of serial killer usually commits murder because of the lust and the thrill of it all, and quite often there's a connection between the violence of the murder and sexual gratification. They think about the murder before they commit it, envisioning in their mind what it will be like. They feel a lot of gratification when their expectations are met. (Jeffrey Dahmer)

Power and Control

This type of serial killer relishes overpowering, dominating, and humiliating the victims and making them feel weak. Often, the serial killer was abused as a child, which left them feeling powerless, something they feel they're getting back with the killings. The victims are usually random and convenient and not someone they know. (Ted Bundy)

Mission

A serial killer who's on a mission believes he is justified in killing certain types of people and doesn't see it as something "wrong." A perfect example of this type of person is Jack the Ripper, who believed killing prostitutes was doing the world a favor or Charles Manson, who was charming and extraordinary at manipulating people and bending them to his will.

Visionary

Visionaries believe someone is whispering in their ear, telling them who they need to kill. They're usually not of sound mind and are psychotic. (David Berkowitz)

A look at several of the most notorious serial killers of all time:

As a disclaimer, some of these examples are detailed and may be difficult/emotional to read …

1. Born in 1946 in England, **Harold Shipman**, a.k.a. Doctor Death, was a general practitioner who killed around 250 people before he was arrested and put away for life. Most of his victims were elderly women. Harold grew up in a Methodist family and was active in sports in his youth, where he excelled as a distance runner and was made vice-captain of the athletic team in high school, even though he was considered to be a loner and had few friends.

    So, what happened?

    One could suggest it had all started in high school when his mother (who was known to be a dominating woman) developed lung cancer. As her condition worsened, she was administered morphine, and even though her condition was terminal, Harold saw how much the morphine made a difference (and later used a similar method with his own patients). She died when he was 17.

Harold went on to marry, have several children, and graduate from medical school. For decades (between 1975-1998) he overdosed his patients, resulting in over 200 murders. Because his victims were older, and many were cremated, he got away with it, even though it eventually came out that he had altered their medical records to suit him and what he'd done.

With some of Harold's patients, it appeared there was monetary gain, such as a woman whose will he altered and forged before her death, or many of his female patients whose jewelry he stole. Much of the rest remains a mystery. As to why Harold did it … he maintained his innocence right up to the time he hung himself in his jail cell. He never confessed to the murders.

Recommended Reading: *Harold Shipman, The True Story of Britain's Most Notorious Serial Killer* by Ryan Green

2. **Belle Gunness** is known as one of the first female black widows. She was born in 1857 in Norway and was the youngest of eight children. Her parents were poor, and life was rough. She moved to America in 1881 seeking wealth and the American Dream.

    At age 25, Belle married her first husband Mads Sorenson who owned a candy store. Soon after, his store burned down as did their home, after which the couple pocketed the insurance money on both. Then Mads mysteriously died. At age 43, Belle married Peter Gunness, a local butcher and widower. He also died under mysterious circumstances, and it was rumored Belle took a meat cleaver and knocked him over the head.

After Peter died, Belle began posting personal ads in the paper, attempting to lure wealthy men to her farmhouse. Many of the men who responded to the ad were never seen or heard from again. In 1908, the Gunness farmhouse burned down. Police found the remains of over 40 people, including Belle's own children and stepchildren. A female body was found without its head, and for a while, it was assumed the body belonged to Belle and that she had perished in the fire. However, Ray Lamphere, Belle's hired hand, claimed Belle had faked her death, cleared her bank account, and taken off. Belle was never found, and to this day, no one knows what happened to her.

When I think of who I consider to be among the evilest serial killers, Belle is at the top of the list. She lacked a conscience, was most likely a psychopath, and had a single motivation in life: money.

Recommended Reading: *Hell's Princess: The Mystery of Belle Gunness, Butcher of Men* by Harold Schechter

3. **Ed Gein**, the inspiration for Norman Bates in the movie *Psycho*, Leatherface in *The Texas Chainsaw Massacre*, and Buffalo Bill in *The Silence of the Lambs*, was born in Wisconsin in 1906 to a shy, alcoholic father and a religious, controlling mother. He was awkward, and his mother's puritanical views on sex and comparing women to prostitutes probably only added to his weirdness.

At the age of nine, Ed's family moved to a farm where he spent the majority of his time when he wasn't in school. When Ed was 34, his father died. Four years later, Ed and his brother were burning some marsh vegetation on the property. The fire spread, and Ed's brother died. Although it was thought to be an accident at the time, Ed was later suspected to have murdered him when an autopsy showed bruising on his brother's head and suggested his brother died *before* the fire had blazed out of control.

Even as an adult, Ed never left the family home. He remained devoted to his mother, and he never dated. His mother died when he was 39, at which point Ed's mental state started to decline. In 1957, Bernice Worden was reported missing. Her son, a deputy sheriff, suspected Ed was involved in her disappearance. A search of his home revealed a gruesome discovery when the deputy found his mother Bernice hanging from the ceiling inside Ed's house. Her head had been removed, and she had been gutted. As if that wasn't enough, various organs were found in jars, along with skulls Ed had eaten out of, death masks, and furniture made from human skin.

Once arrested, Ed confessed to murdering two women, and he said many of the organs he'd collected over the years had come from bodies he'd exhumed at the cemetery. He was found not guilty by way of insanity and diagnosed with schizophrenia. The remainder of his life was spent in a mental hospital until his death in 1984.

Recommended Reading: *Deviant: True Story of Ed Gein, the Original Psycho* by Harold Schechter

4. Born in Illinois in 1942 to a blue-collar family, **John Wayne Gacy** murdered at least 33 males during his killing spree and buried 26 of them in the crawl space beneath his house. But before we get into what he did, let's discuss his backstory and uncover how John turned into a notorious serial killer in the first place.

As a boy, John's alcoholic father beat him, his mother, and his siblings if he believed they had misbehaved. On one occasion, John's father struck him on the head with a broomstick, leaving him unconscious. His father was verbally abusive as well, often telling John he was dumb, a sissy, and stupid. And given John had a congenial heart condition, his father made fun of him and saw him as weak. And that's not all. At the tender age of seven, John began being molested by a family friend who sometimes gave him a ride.

As John aged, he realized he was attracted to men, but sadly, he lived in a day and age where it wasn't accepted in society, and because of this, he was ashamed of his feelings. When John was 26, he was sent to prison for ten years for sexually assaulting two teenage boys. He served two years, was released on parole, and was charged with the same crime a year later. That particular teen didn't show up for trial, and the case was dropped.

In his 30s, John was a well-liked businessman who ran a construction business and hosted parties for his entire neighborhood. He even became a Democratic precinct captain. He was married twice and fathered two children. In 1975, he confessed to his second wife that he was bisexual, and that same year, she filed for divorce.

In 1978, when John was 36, Robert Piest went missing. Several days later, police found evidence of John's crimes and learned John had been murdering men since he was 30. He received the nickname "Killer Clown" because he was a member of the "Jolly Joker" clown club, performed as a clown, and sometimes dressed up as Pogo the Clown when he killed his victims.

Once he was arrested for multiple murders, John confessed to killing 30 people. He was found guilty, and he died in 1994 at the age of 52.

Recommended Reading: *Killer Clown* by Terry Sullivan

5. **Jeffrey Dahmer** was born in Wisconsin in 1970. At the age of four he underwent surgery for a double hernia. His parents argued a lot and engaged in vicious fights throughout his childhood. His father was away a lot, and his mother suffered from anxiety and was a hypochondriac in constant need of attention. Eventually, his mother had an affair, and his parents divorced.

Jeffrey's thoughts first turned to murder when he was 14. At the same age, he began drinking heavily, which resulted in an alcoholism problem he would battle for years to come. At age 18, he enlisted in the Army as a medical specialist. He served a short three years and then was released.

Let's back up a few years to Jeffrey's first murder. At the age of 18, before his enlistment to the military, Jeffrey picked up a hitchhiker, killed him, and then buried him beneath his parents' home. He didn't kill again for nine years, but between the years of 1981 and 1989, he was arrested four times for disorderly conduct, indecent exposure, and sexual crimes.

Between the years of 1989 and 1991, Jeffrey committed another 13 murders. He lured victims to his home and promised them money and sex. Once there, he tainted their alcohol with drugs and strangled them. He then would take Polaroid photos of his victims so he could relive his crimes, and similar to fellow serial killer Ed Gein, he kept various body parts of his victims as souvenirs.

In 1991, one of his would-be victim's escaped. When the police went to Jeffrey's home, they found Polaroid pictures of dismembered bodies, and he was arrested. He pled guilty initially and then changed his plea to guilty by virtue of insanity. It didn't take the jury long to find him guilty, but his prison time was short lived. A couple of years after his conviction, he was murdered by a fellow inmate.

Recommended Reading: *The Jeffrey Dahmer Story: An American Nightmare* by Donald A. Davis

6. **Ted Bundy** admitted to killing 36 women, but it's been suspected the actual number of victims is well over 100. Born in Vermont in 1946 in a home for unwed mothers, Ted never knew the identity of his biological father. His religious grandparents raised him as their adopted son and told him his mother was his sister. That lie, in itself, messed him up.

It's believed Ted's first murder occurred in 1974 when he was 28 years old. That's around the time several women in Oregon and Seattle went missing. He was kind when approaching his victims, often feigning an injury and asking for help or posing as an authority figure. He was an attractive, charismatic man, which made the women he stalked easy prey (although I've always felt when you look in his eyes in various photos of him that there's an obvious look of madness, one you'd often see in sociopaths).

Ted was intelligent and even had a psychology degree. When it came time for his trial, he chose to represent himself, but he was still found guilty. He said he felt no remorse for what he'd done.

During his time in prison, Ted escaped twice, but since his face was sensationalized on the news and in papers everywhere, it was never long before he was found. He was executed in the electric chair in 1989 at the age of 43.

Recommended Reading: *The Stranger Beside Me* by Anne Rule, a woman who had once been Ted's friend.

7. No serial killer list would be complete unless it included **Jack the Ripper**, a man shrouded in mystery. Who was he? To this day, we're not 100% certain, and back when the murders occurred, there were over 100 suspects.

What we do know about Jack is that his crime spree took place in London in 1888. He murdered at least five female prostitutes, and the murders all took place within one mile of each other. He was suspected to have sent several letters to police at the time, teasing them about the murders he'd committed and the murders still to come. Forensics wasn't what it is today, after all, so police were unsuccessful in using the letters to figure out the Ripper's identity. The strangest part about the murders is that after his initial killing spree, they just stopped, which is odd for a serial killer. To this day, no one knows why.

Recommended Reading: *Portrait of a Killer* by Patricia Cornwell (which only appears to be available in paperback or hardback at the moment). As a side note, I've read this book and Cornwell has me convinced that she's cracked the case as to the mystery of Jack the Ripper's true identity. She's written two follow-up books which are excellent as well: *Chasing the Ripper* and *Ripper: The Secret Life of Walter Sickert.*

8. We round off the list of notable serial killers with the ghastly **H.H. Holmes**, the "Beast of Chicago" and his murder castle. Herman Webster Mudgett (who later took on the alias Dr. Henry Howard Holmes) was born in New Hampshire in 1861 to strict Methodist parents. His mother was said to be a cold, distant individual, and his father was an alcoholic. There are stories about Herman being physically and verbally abused by his demanding parents, which included forcing their son to be alone for long periods of time and depriving him of food.

At the age of 17, he married Clara Levering, but the marriage lasted only a year before he left her. He enrolled in the University of Michigan's Department of Medicine and Surgery program and graduated in 1884. He moved to Chicago the following year and found work at a pharmacy. During this time, he acquired a piece of land and had a three-story home built. The first floor was the pharmacy, and the second and third floors contained apartments. But they weren't your run-of-the-mill apartments. Some of the rooms in the house were soundproof and had trapdoors.

It's believed the murders started in the early part of the 1890s during the Columbian Exposition. He tricked naïve, unsuspecting people into staying at his house, which he said was a hotel. He was arrested in 1894 for selling mortgaged goods, was released, and then continued killing until the police caught up to him again. He confessed to 27 murders, although some believe the real number of victims is as high as 200. He was hung in 1896.

Recommended Reading: *The Devil in the White City*, by Erik Larson, which is being turned into a Hulu Miniseries.

Writing about real-life serial killers is a bit disturbing. In the examples above I tried to deliver factual tidbits without going into too many graphic details. More specific information can be found in the books I recommended above.

And now let's all take in a deep breath and move on from all of this heaviness!

<u>Serial killers vs. mass murderers vs. spree killers</u>

A mass murderer is someone who commits several murders at one time. They are the type of people who walk into a movie theater or onto a college campus and just start shooting. Spree killers are similar in that they might murder a mass of people, but it will be at two or more locations, one right after the other.

<u>A villain of a different variety:</u>

Villains come in all shapes and sizes, and they're all unique in their own way. Let's discuss some of the more common ones used on the movie/TV screen and in today's fiction.

The Prodigal Son/Black Sheep
This kind of villain has usually been born with wealth and

privilege and with an innate desire to make mommy and daddy proud. Somewhere along the line, he learns his parents aren't proud, and no matter what he does to try and prove his worth, they never will be. He is resentful and bitter, but he takes his ball and goes home … until one day he snaps and the pent-up anger releases in a huge tidal wave of bad choices. For a great example of this on multiple levels, watch the HBO series *Succession*. It's one of the best shows I've ever seen on this type of villain.

The Desperado

Desperados are often on the run from the crimes they've committed, or they are someone who has found themselves trapped in a world of the poor choices they've made. Their main goal in life is to live another day (no matter what the cost) without getting caught, and they will do whatever it takes to ensure that happens. They may not want to kill, but when it comes down to it, they will when they don't feel they have any other choice.

The Fake Friend

The fake friend wants something and if feigning their love and admiration for a person will help them achieve those goals, they'll do whatever it takes to succeed. This type of villain always makes me think of Rebecca De Mornay in the movie *The Hand that Rocks the Cradle*. In the movie, De Mornay plays a nanny who's out to destroy the baby's mother, seduce the father, and keep the father and the baby for herself.

The Red is for Revenge

Revenge killers are motivated to exact their own justice, a justice they don't believe they'll get any other way. Think of the swoon-worthy Keanu Reeves' character in *John Wick* after guys break into his house, steal his car, and kill his dog. To John, there's only one option here. The men must be found, and they must die.

Period. Other examples of this kind of killer are The Bride in *Kill Bill* and Liam Neeson as Brian Mills in the movie *Taken*.

The Mastermind

This villain usually has it out for the protagonist and wants to oppose them and be one step ahead of them at all times. Think of Mads Mikkelsen's character Le Chiffre against James Bond in *Casino Royale*. They are the brain, not the brawn, and they make great villains in spy-type stories.

Anti-Hero

Who doesn't love a good anti-hero? I shouldn't like that Jeff Lindsay's famed character Dexter goes around murdering people according to a code his father raised him with, where it's really not okay to kill but some people actually make the cut (pun intended). Murder is murder, right? Wrong. Dexter is a great example of a character that has sway over readers because of all the other things about him that readers find likable and human. Another great example is Sir Anthony Hopkins' character in Thomas Harris' book *The Silence of The Lambs*. He is evil in his way, but his father-figure relationship with Clarice Starling allows us to feel sympathy for him.

The Femme Fatale

When I think of an example of a femme fatale, one woman comes to mind over all others: Sharon Stone in her role of Catherine Tramell in the movie *Basic Instinct*. (As a side note, I'm starting to feel like I'm aging myself here with some of these older film examples! But hey, oldies are goodies.)

Now then ... a femme fatale has mastered one thing above all others—the art of seduction. She's so skilled at it, when men and women get trapped in her web, it leads to their downfall. What's fun about writing this kind of character is you can make the women slightly evil/bad people who readers still connect with on some level, or you can go the other direction and make them a full super villain.

The Equal

Equals may be similar to your protagonist. Maybe they went to school together, had the same middle-class upbringing and similar opportunities, but the line is drawn when one chooses to do what's right and the other chooses to do what's wrong. One great example is the relationship between Professor X and Magneto in *X-Men*. The pair weren't always enemies.

The Bully

We all know what a bully is, so this one speaks for itself. Bullies usually behave the way they do because they were bullied or are being bullied, or they're just mean, horrendous people. Some serial killer characters can fall into this category, and normal people can fall into it as well. Think Rachel McAdams in *Mean Girls*, The Heathers in *Heathers*, and spoiled Nellie Oleson on *Little House on the Prairie*.

The Criminal

Criminals are your mafia types, the people who commit crimes because there's something in it for them, which usually involves money or power or both. They make decisions to benefit themselves and those they love first and foremost, and the consequences of their actions come second. Sometimes they're endearing characters like mafia boss Tony Soprano in *The Sopranos* or Jax Teller and Gemma Teller in *Sons of Anarchy*.

The Henchman

Henchmen do the dirty deed so their boss doesn't have to get his own hands dirty. They're the brawn attached to the person they work for, who is the brain. They tend to be ruthless and usually have no problem doing what they're told, no matter how arduous the task seems. They tend to be a simpler character compared to the main villain in the story. Good examples of this type of person would be Lenny Montana's character in *The Godfather* and Count Tyron Rugen from *The Princess Bride*.

The Corrupted

Villains who are corrupted generally started out as good people and then became tainted somewhere along the way and switch from good to bad. This includes people of power, such as politicians or people in police/FBI/detective positions. The main person who comes to mind in this category is Jack Nicholson's character Jack Torrance in Stephen King's *The Shining*. In a more recent series, the character Walter White in *Breaking Bad*, who could be in the anti-hero category as well.

The Disturbed/Fanatic

These are your serial killers and any character who's not right in the head and has some kind of mental disorder which alters the way they think. They give themselves a free pass for their actions because they believe they are fulfilling a moral obligation. They usually have bizarre personality quirks and are way outside of what's considered to be "the norm" of society. They are unpredictable, which is one of the reasons they make for such meaty, rich characters. Think of Ethan Hawke's character Costa in the movie *Taking Lives* and Leonardo DiCaprio's character Teddy Daniels in *Shutter Island*.

<u>Why do people kill?</u>

Since the theme of our books is murder, it's good to know what drives people to commit the acts they do. Below is a short list of some of the main reasons.

- Jealousy
- Revenge
- Justice
- Fear
- Mental Issues
- Money
- Desperation

CHAPTER 12

DOOR NO. 1, 2, OR 3: SUSPECTS AND RED HERRINGS

red herring *(n) a clue or piece of information which is or is intended to be misleading or distracting.*

R ed herrings are diversions meant to lead readers in a different direction, taking them off the initial path of the investigation and sending them on a different one where they'll ask themselves questions like, "What if it could be him instead of her?"

Red herrings aren't the real culprits.

They're innocent suspects swept up in a situation they may have some connection to, but they're *not* the murderers … and they're also not always people.

<u>A few examples of common red herrings</u>:

- An event that held meaning for the protagonist
- A character who has done something to raise suspicion
- A clue placed in the right place at the right time to lead the investigator down a path that goes nowhere
- An item or object left at the scene or in a place of significance that suggests it's tied to the murder when it isn't

"Red herrings are well-crafted plot twists."

Quite simply, red herrings are well-crafted plot twists. They're how we keep the reader guessing until the bitter, breathtaking end. Craft them well and your reader will be delightfully surprised and satisfied when they reach the end of the novel.

Red herrings are essential to mystery fiction. If these essential characters/situations didn't exist, cases wouldn't have as much depth and substance. Stories would also be over too quickly, something a reader never wants. We also don't want the reader to catch on too fast. When they do, it's like a deflated balloon. Once the air is out, the excitement is over.

When readers are thrown off course, they question everything about what they *thought* they knew up to that point in the story. Readers want to believe they have things all figured out. When they realize they don't, it reinvigorates them to continue on with the story, put their thinking caps on, and guess again. It's part of the thrill, and it's a thrill they must have in order to be satisfied.

How do we write red herrings in a way that's plausible without taking away from the story itself?

<u>Here are a handful of suggestions I've seen used most often:</u>

- Have the protagonist discover a new clue which turns out to be conflicting evidence and steers him/her away from what they'd previously believed. The clue then turns out to be nothing, shifting the focus back to the original clue the protagonist had focused on (or before the new twist).
- Introduce a new character who is innocent but tied to the crime somehow or one that has a possible motive to murder.
- Make something seem shady that ends up being no big deal at all. Example: an earring found in the bachelor pad at the crime scene ends up being one the victim's mother lost the last time she had visited her son.
- Have the innocent victim appear guilty at first.

A red herring as a character should be one who either benefits from the crime in some way, has the opportunity to commit the crime, is present before, during or after the crime, or has a reason to commit the crime.

Example: A woman dies and shortly thereafter everyone learns her husband changed her life insurance policy prior to her death.

Example: A woman is seen arguing with a man at a restaurant. She says, "I wish you were dead!" Three hours later, he's murdered.

Example: A neighbor sees a woman run out of the house with a bloody knife, but it turns out she only had the knife in her hand because she'd arrived to visit her mother-in-law and found her dead in the living room with the bloody knife next to her body.

- Throw the reader off by entering a character into the story that seems to be a logical match for the murderer they're looking for, even though he's innocent.

Red herrings should have some tie to the murder, even if it's minor, and a motive which makes the reader believe that character could be involved somehow.

Mystery readers expect red herrings in the stories, and they welcome them as long as they are plausibly written.

Red herrings also allow you to plant clues in a nonchalant way while you direct attention to something or someone else. By creating a good distraction, you can insert a clue into a scene where it appears to mean nothing … until it does.

Interested in a little more research on this topic? Consider reading *And Then There Were None* by Agatha Christie.

CHAPTER 13

THOU SHALT NOT: NEEDLESSLY HARMING PETS/ CHILDREN

I want to start off this chapter by saying that I'm not here to tell you what to do. It's your book. Do what you want with it. I am here to advise, and if I didn't at least discuss this topic, I would be doing you a disservice. Once you have the information, then you can decide what to do with it.

Our demographic is largely the 50+ crowd. Why? They read more in our genre and are either empty nesters or have older children, are heading toward retirement or are already there—and simply put, they have more free time. At the moment, my readers tend to be a bit more conservative than readers of other genres, but I believe I'll see a shift in that over the next ten years, and I have already seen a shift from 2011 to now. What a difference a decade can make, right?

Let's say your protagonist has a cute, adorable dog as a sidekick in your series. In my Sloane Monroe series, I have Lord Berkeley, a.k.a. Boo, a westie who's featured in several books in the series. In a few of my books, I left him out, and I have received emails over that from readers who want him in every book they read. They miss him when he's not part of the story.

I've also added a dog to my new series—Luka, a beautiful, protective Samoyed. If I did anything to harm Luka or Boo in an offensive way, I have no doubt I'd lose a small percentage of my reader base EVEN IF they'd read and loved my books. Boo is getting up there in age. He's eleven this year, which means he won't be around for too many more years. When he passes, I will write about it in a humane, sensitive way, giving readers the chance to mourn him.

When it comes to doggos and kiddos (and cats) many readers have a zero-tolerance policy. I can write a book where the killer goes on a murderous crime spree, but if a single hair on a pet or child's head is missing, the gloves come off, and they'll make sure I hear about it. In the movie *John Wick*, Keanu Reeves' character is so pissed off about the men who had murdered his dog, he sets out to kill every single person who was involved. He becomes enraged, and while we sit and watch with our eyes glued to the screen and our hands dipped into buttered popcorn, we become enraged too.

Are there exceptions to this though?

Definitely.

John Wick is the perfect example because we are horrified to learn the dog died. When Wick grabs his gun and heads out to retaliate, he isn't just getting justice for himself. He's getting justice for us too.

When writing about kids, it's all about how you craft the situation in your story. For example, in my novel *Bed of Bones*, the book begins with two young brothers wandering around an area next to an abandoned mine shaft in Park City, Utah, an area their parents have forbidden them to be in. The younger of the two is playing around the opening of the shaft with his Slinky. He drops it. It tumbles toward the open mine shaft and falls in. Without thinking, the boy races to retrieve it. He slips, falls into the mine, and dies. The scene is now set for the rest of the story, and when the police repel down the shaft to recover his body, they discover the bodies of several missing women.

What happened to the boy was tragic, but unlike the women who were murdered, the boy's death was nothing more than an unfortunate accident, and readers tend to be a lot more forgiving when it's written that way. I took this into consideration when I wrote the scene, and I crossed all my fingers and toes that it would be well received by readers. To date, *Bed of Bones* is one of my most downloaded books and has 3,600 four-and-five-star reviews between Amazon, Barnes & Noble, Apple Books, and Kobo. This tells me I can write something similar in the future, and odds are it will be accepted as well. Yaaaas!

"One of the best pieces of advice I can give you is to know your audience."

One of the best pieces of advice I can give you is to know your audience. Know them inside and out. Know what they like and what they don't like. Know what makes them pick up a book and what makes them put it down.

In summary, be compassionate when writing about children and pets. It's a fine line you need to consider before you cross it—if you do.

CHAPTER 14

EXIT STAGE LEFT: LEAVING SEX AT THE DOOR

Can your characters have sex scenes or romantic relationships in your story?

Yep, they can.

Should sex scenes be described in detail or written as a major theme in a mystery or thriller book?

Nope.

We're mystery, thriller, and suspense writers, not romance and erotica authors. Our readers are here because they're interested in the crime that has been committed, and they want to come along for the ride as we work together to solve it. If they wanted page after page of passionate, raw romantic interludes, they'd skip mysteries and read another genre. They come to us and our books because we offer something different, and we should.

I almost always include romantic relationships in my books. As long as they don't overshadow the murder investigation, they make for lovely subplots and add to the depth of the main character. I'll even throw in a kiss or three, a hug, the odd tender caress, and sweet, sweet nothings here and there, but I *do not* add much more beyond that. It's possible to put two people in a room together and make it obvious that they're about to have sex without spelling it out. Readers in our genre are smart. Trust me ... they "get it."

How I choose to incorporate romantic relationships in my books works well for me, but you're not me, so it's smart to consider how readers feel about it nowadays. No matter what we think about what should or shouldn't be included in our stories, the opinion of our readers is what we should be thinking about.

On that note, I polled a group of mystery readers and asked them to weigh in on the subject. In the poll, readers were given four choices, and this is how they voted:

- I'm okay with romance and a bit of sex in novels as long as it's tasteful. 72%
- I'm okay with romance as long as sex is kept at the door. 15%
- I'm okay with sex scenes even if they're graphic. 12%
- I'm not okay with sex scenes. 1%

Those questioned were primarily women aged 40+. From the poll, we can see more mystery readers are becoming comfortable with us including sex in our novels as long as it isn't graphic, but I was surprised to see that 12% are still fine with the graphic stuff too. It goes to show how much things have changed over the last decade when writing heavy sex scenes in our genre was frowned upon.

What did some of the readers I polled have to say? Let's find out ...

"I have no problem with short, tastefully written sex scenes. When the scene goes on and on, I skip ahead to get back to the mystery."
Sarah D.

"I guess it depends on whether the book is a 'mystery' or a 'cozy mystery,' but I prefer the focus to be on the mystery itself." Sharyn B.

"Tasteful. No erotica. Just normal monkey sex. Not circus." Caroline D.

"If there is sexual tension that is finally resolved, that is fine. But I don't want it as the major focus." Sheri P.

"I do like to see some romance in my mystery stories. As for sex, as long as it's tasteful and brief, I don't mind." Christine P.

"Sometimes just the hint of it or having sex off-screen is all the story needs." Lorne O.

"Unless you're writing a cozy mystery, don't skip the sex scenes. I personally feel like they add to the chemistry and dynamic between characters, but I am an eclectic reader." Leah H.

"For me, sex scenes and sometimes the sexual tension between the two characters leading up to the actual sex scene can give us an insight into the characters, adding another dimension to them." Dorothy B.

"I like romance between characters but would rather leave more to the imagination than having it all in graphic words." Jean M.

"I am okay with some tasteful sex scenes as long as they are important to the story. In a casual situation or a one-night stand, I do not want to read sex scenes. For developing a solid relationship, it adds to the story." Carol C.

"I don't like graphic sex scenes. I prefer scenes that leave something to the imagination." Susan R.

"I'm fine with sex scenes in mystery novels. It's a normal part of life." Sharon B.

"I don't mind romance in mystery novels, but I have no desire to read sex scenes." Sandra S.

"Tasteful is fine, though I would just as soon not read about the specific moves or body parts involved." Lois B.

"I have no problem with short, tastefully-written sex scenes. When the scene goes on and on, I skip ahead to get back to the mystery." Sarah D.

"People have sex. It's part of life. I don't need the details. I have an imagination." DorieLou S.

"I think it takes away from the mystery and cheapens it. I can buy a Harper romance book if I want that." Kimberly D.

"As long as it isn't an entire chapter long, there's nothing wrong with sex scenes in a mystery novel." KaLynne L.

"I'm okay with it as long as it goes with the novel and is not just there for gratuitous sex." Susanne T.

"I read mystery novels because they are mystery novels. If one wants to read graphic sex scenes, they should buy books in another genre." Renata J.

"Mystery in a novel keeps the reader intrigued, as does the romance if it's interspersed in the story and can add another element that doesn't take away from the actual story." Kim O.

"Alluding to a sexual encounter without being blatant adds a bit of spice and can aid a good mystery." Sandra B.

"I like mysteries with a hint of romance." Stephanie S.

"A little romance and tasteful sex are okay, but I read mystery novels for the mystery and intrigue and not for the romance and sex." Dorothy L.

"I enjoy mysteries with a touch of romance. The problem is when it ends up taking over the mystery. I have read some mysteries where the romance takes over and they never got back to solving the mystery until the very end. It's very frustrating." Shannon C.

"If the scene is too explicit, I skip a few pages." Sandra P.

"It doesn't need to be described in detail. If an author says the characters are 'passionately kissing,' that's all that needs to be said." Laurie D.

CHAPTER 15

ANATOMY OF A MURDER: WRITING A GREAT MURDER SCENE

I've previously mentioned that you want your murder to take place as early as possible in your novel—and specifically within the first few chapters of the book. Now let's go over what needs to be conveyed to the reader when the murder takes place.

The most important thing I can say here is to <u>get your facts straight</u>. I'd write that statement in all caps, but I don't want to yell. Do not give your readers a reason to complain about something you said that isn't factual. This is especially true when it comes to assessing time of death or anything forensics related. If you're not sure, either take the time to learn it, or leave it out, though if you're going to be a mystery writer, you should learn as much as you can about forensics because it makes a big difference when writing those scenes.

I have read several books on forensics, which I'll list at the end of this book in the Recommended Reads section, but the best thing I've ever done for myself was to create a notebook where I alphabetically listed out the different things I'd learned during my research on forensics. I refresh it now and then when I can, print it out, put it in a plastic sleeve, and keep it next to me so I can refer to it when necessary.

Other than books, I watched the hell out of the series *Forensic Files*. Whenever something was said of interest, I jotted it down and added it to the notebook. I am particularly interested in unique situations that aren't overused in novels.

<u>Here's an example of the first few items in my notebook:</u>

Amido Black (*Forensic Files*, Episode: Pressed for Crime)
Amido black can be sprayed on something to reveal a print, like a shoe print. It reacts to the dried blood left at the crime scene and can reveal a foot impression that can give the size of the shoe the killer was wearing, and often the type of shoe they were wearing as well. After it's applied, the impression appears in seconds.

Blood on Carpeting (*Forensic Files*, Episode: Best Foot Forward)
When stains that may be blood are found on a rug or section of carpet, the forensics examiner can mark it with a grid of four-inch squares. Each square is swabbed with phenolphthalein and hydrogen peroxide, a chemical combination that turns pink when it comes into contact with blood. A pattern will emerge that creates an outline of human blood, and this can be tested for DNA.

Beating (*Forensic Files*, Episode: Hell's Kitchen)
Whenever a beating takes place and blood comes to the surface, subsequent blows start to disperse the blood and it causes blood to be spattered onto the surrounding surfaces. If the police find a body in a bathroom, but there's no blood spatter after a physical assault that drew blood, they know the victim was not killed where he/she was found, and the law enforcement needs to search the house and surrounding area for the exact spot the murder took place.

These notes have really helped me when I need to refer back to something I'm writing about. Including where I'd found the information, especially when it comes to television episodes, makes it easy for me to refer to the episode if I need to brush up on what I'd watched for a scene I'm writing.

Let's switch gears and talk about how to write a riveting murder scene. There are a lot of different ways writers can establish the who, what, why, when, and how of what happened to the victim.

"Make sure the murder is realistic."

<u>Tips on writing a great murder scene</u>:

1. Make sure the murder is realistic.

2. Once you've chosen the method of murder, give it an accurate, believable timeline.

    For example, let's say the victim was poisoned. Some poisons cause death right away. Others take several hours to kick in.

    This can also be applied to other types of murder.

    A bullet to the head will be instantaneous in most cases, whereas a bullet to the chest will differ depending on what part of the chest was affected.

Whichever way the victim is murdered, make 100% certain it's accurate to the method you choose.

3. The time of death is almost always an estimate.

    Realistic time of death: He died within the last two hours.

    Unrealistic time of death: He died at 8:07 p.m.

    Why? There's no way to be that accurate unless the victim's watch was, say, smashed at the exact time of death and stopped working, and even then, the victim could have kept breathing for a while before taking his/her final breath.

4. Make sure your terminology is right. There are many great articles on this subject on the internet.

5. Understand the crime scene.

    Crime scenes are usually secure locations where gloves and other protective gear are worn as evidence is being collected. Most characters shouldn't be able to waltz right in if they're not with the police, unless it's in a special circumstance.

6. Lab results take time.

    You need to allow for this.

    You don't send something to the lab and have the results back within a few minutes. In reality, it takes a lot longer to process evidence than the timeline of the book from beginning to end, and readers understand that to a certain degree.

One workaround I've found is to have my detectives have a personal relationship/friendship with the ME (medical examiner) or coroner so it's more plausible for them to get results a bit faster than they normally would.

CHAPTER 16

I Spy with my Little Eye: The Investigation

The investigation should take up the bulk of your story. But first, there needs to be a strong, compelling murder to hook readers and keep them hanging on from start to finish.

Why do people kill in the first place?

What motivates them to do it?

We've been over this a bit in previous chapters, but let's get a bit more specific.

<u>The main reasons people commit murder:</u>

Money
This could be anything from robbery to killing someone to get the insurance money.

Hatred

The killer feels they have been wronged in some way and despises the other individual enough to end his life. This would be something like a father learning his daughter's boyfriend has physically abused her and becomes angered to the point of ending the boyfriend's life.

Mental Illness

The crime is committed by someone who is mentally unstable and may not even understand what they have done to the full extent.

This "mental illness" can be a bit of a hard sell most of the time, by the way. Just because people "buy it" in a movie doesn't mean readers will "buy it" on the page. I've often found writers can't get away with some of the things that regularly occur in movies and television shows.

Mistaken Identity

The killer murders the wrong person such as the brother of the intended target, a twin, or someone he thought wronged him, only to realize he'd made a mistake.

Sympathy

A nurse ends the life of a terminal patient to ease their pain and suffering (this is not common in murder mysteries).

Crime of Passion

A woman learns her sister has been sleeping with her husband and kills them both.

Jealousy

A man breaks things off with his wife and starts seeing another woman. The wife, who is still in love with him, can't handle him being with anyone other than her, so she kills him because she'd rather he was dead than with another person.

Revenge

This is probably my favorite one because there are so many ways to spin it. One example would be a high school girl gets raped by several members of the football team. Several years later, she is still so scarred by what happened, she decides to start picking off her rapists one by one.

To Cover Up Another Crime

Maybe the VP of a big company has been embezzling money, and the secretary just found out about what he's done. He kills her to keep her quiet.

Secrets

This is my other favorite one to write about because secrets make for good twists in stories and are usually shocking.

Obsession

A lot of your serial-killer murders fall into this category where the killer has a fascination with women with long dark hair or men or couples hanging out on lover's lane, etc.

"Make your readers a promise. Once it's made, be sure to deliver on that promise."

At the start of the story, it's our job to invite the reader in and help them get comfortable so they become emotionally invested in what's going on. Essentially, we're luring them inside by saying, "Come on in: the water's warm. You'll love it."

We're making them a promise. And once it's made, it's time to deliver.

Jane Doe has been murdered, and it's up to your savvy sleuth (FBI person, police officer, detective, cat sleuth, etc.) to figure out *who* committed the crime and *why* the crime was committed.

The first job for any sleuth is to visit the scene of the crime and to gather information to form a timeline of what happened and the manner in which the events occurred.

Once the evidence is gathered, dissected, and it begins to be processed, the sleuth shifts gears and focuses on the witnesses and the suspects relevant to the case—anyone who may have relevant information.

A handful of suspects is all you need here. Don't spread yourself thin with ten potential suspects. This makes it too complicated for your reader, and if they get too frustrated, they'll give up on your book altogether, no matter how good it may be.

Instead of sending the reader in every possible direction, consider tackling suspects either one at a time, or focus most of your interest on one subject while beginning to have suspicions about another. Think about it like dropping breadcrumbs. If the crumbs are scattered, the reader becomes lost. It's better to make a trail along which they can follow.

As suspects are vetted, false leads and red herrings are eliminated until, at long last, the sleuth has a clear path leading to the true killer. But wait! Let's back up a minute and talk about what's going on behind the scenes while the investigation takes its course.

In a majority of mystery novels, there are two things in play:

1. The investigation, which has a beginning, middle, and end. By the end of the book, the case is solved, and there are no plot holes or unresolved issues.

2. The sleuth's personal life. Although the investigation takes center stage, the sleuth is usually dealing with

their own personal issue as well. This could be something from the past or present that rears its ugly head during the story. These issues are not always 100% resolved, but they change over the course of the story, and by the end, your sleuth has usually changed in some way because of it. This could be anything from a divorce they're going through, an addiction they can't kick, an ex they're not over, the loss of a family member they're still haunted by, etc.

The killing floor

How soon the murder takes place is up to you, but I'd recommend it's within the first three chapters and preferably in chapter one.

In my own books, the murder almost always takes place in chapter one, and it's written in third person from the victim's POV. This formula has worked great for me over the years, and is something my readers have come to expect, which is why I continue writing this way.

There are two common ways for the murder to present itself:

1.   The story opens, and the victim is already dead.
In this scenario, the sleuth works backward to figure out what happened, who the suspects are and why, and what the motive was for the victim's death.
2.   The story opens, and the soon-to-be victim is still alive.
In this scenario, you want to be sure not to keep them alive for too long. If you drag it out, you run the risk of your reader becoming bored and putting the book down.

Remember, the reader wants to take the journey with your sleuth and discover clues along the way. Don't rob them of this opportunity.

How many murders are too many?

The murder has occurred.

Now what?

How long do you need to wait until there's a second victim and a third?

How many victims is *too* many?

If you're writing fantasy books about zombies or epic horror fiction like Stephen King, the more murders the merrier.

For the genres we write in, we want a story that doesn't get too congested for the reader. The last thing you want is for the reader to be so confused they need to go back and read something again and again before they have a handle on what's happening.

The main victim is the primary focus of the story. The secondary victims are an accessory and serve to enhance the primary story. Once you get this down, you're on track to write a successful suspense novel.

CHAPTER 17

PICK YOUR POISON: THE MURDER WEAPON

There are four main ways in which people die: Naturally, Murder, Accidentally, and Suicide.

Since we're writing about murder, that's our main focus.

There are a multitude of ways to kill off your innocents in a novel, including:

- Drowning
- Suffocating/Smothering
- Fire (asphyxiation)
- Beating to death
- Burying alive
- Poisoning
- Shooting
- Stabbing
- Hanging

- Running over
- Pushing (in front of train, etc.)
- Strangling
- Starvation
- Blowing up

No matter which method you choose, the murder itself must be believable. I know I keep saying that, but it's honestly one of the main staples in getting a mystery novel right.

In order for the murder method to be believable, you need to learn about and understand the finer things about your chosen method. You need to know things like the odds of your victim dying when he/she is shot in the chest. When it comes to bullet wounds, the location of the wound makes all the difference.

In addition, like I mentioned before, you also need to know how long it would take for the victim to die, so you get the timeline of the murder right.

The same can be said for offing your victim by way of poison. Poisons are different from each other. Some kill instantly, and others leave the victim writhing for days in agony before death occurs.

Let's focus on the main methods of murder in mystery novels, which are shooting, stabbing, and poison.

Shooting

If your villain is wielding a gun, the first thing you'll need to decide is what kind of gun he has and understand how grave the injury will be once the gun is fired. But even before that, you'll need to get a grasp of basic gun terminology. I'll discuss the basics below and then refer you to a couple of websites and a book every mystery/thriller/suspense author should have in their library.

To begin, bullets, calibers, and cartridges aren't the same thing.

Bullets exit the barrel when the firearm is fired. They're the piece of lead or copper in a rifled barrel. They are one component of the cartridge, the metal projectile that's fired from the gun at high speed.

Cartridges are complete packages that are made up of four things: the case, primer, propellant, and projectile. They include the shell and the bullet.

Caliber refers to the size of the bullet's diameter, which is usually in millimeter form or hundredths of an inch.

<u>Magazine vs. clip:</u>
Magazines look like rectangular-shaped boxes. They hold the cartridge and slide into the end of the semi-automatic pistol. The magazine holds the shells under a spring pressure, which then goes into the chamber of the firearm.

Clips do not have springs. They hold cartridges, and once the round has been fired, the clip can be released, and the gun can be reloaded.

<u>**Types of guns:**</u>

- Shotguns
- Handguns
- Rifles

<u>Shotguns:</u>
Shotguns are two-handed firearms. They have a smooth bore that is not rifled. They are better at shooting close-range at targets less than

50 yards away. Squeeze a shotgun's trigger, and multiple projectiles are fired (though they're nothing like machine guns).

Handguns can be fired with a single hand, although they can be fired using two hands for added stability.

Handguns come in two types: pistols and revolvers.

Pistols are single-barrel handguns that have a chamber which is integral with its barrel.

Revolvers are aptly named because their cartridges are inside a revolving cylinder. They are not loaded by magazines but by stripper clips instead.

A rifle is a long firearm that you fire a single bullet from. It has "rifling," which are patterned grooves that cause the bullet to spin when it's fired, allowing for a much more accurate shot. They are heavier than shotguns and can hit long-distance targets 75-100 yards away.

Automatic weapon vs. semi-automatic weapon

With an automatic weapon, you pull the trigger once and it releases a lot of rounds.

With a semi-automatic, one pull of the trigger releases one round, but you can keep pulling the trigger to release more rounds.

A few final comments with regards to using firearms. Make sure the firearm you use suits the crime. For example, if the victim is a thousand yards away, getting shot by a 9mm gun isn't realistic. You'd want to use a high-power rifle instead.

One of the other mistakes I see all the time in fiction, even by big-name authors, is when they talk about removing the safety. Not all handguns have external safeties! One easy way to avoid this in writing if you aren't sure is not to get too technical or specific about the firearm in the first place.

And finally, avoid having the assailant turn the firearm sideways in some kind of a "thug life" maneuver and then expect the bullet to magically hit the target. Why? It's unrealistic! Sights on the top of firearms are there for a reason.

A great book on firearms and knives that every author should have in their arsenal is *The Writer's Guide to Weapons: A Practical Reference for Using Firearms and Knives in Fiction* by Benjamin Sobieck and David Morrell.

Stabbing

Most of the time stabbing homicides are the result of knife wounds, but people can be attacked with all kinds of things: pencil, fork, scissors, screwdriver, sword, poker, ice pick. This is a great opportunity to get creative in your books.

Stab wounds are either slash wounds, puncture wounds, chopping wounds, or incision wounds—for our purposes, that's *puncture*, *chop*, or *slash*.

Puncture wounds penetrate more deeply than slash wounds and have a much greater chance of harming body organs.

When the body is examined after a stabbing, the medical examiner tries to identify the track marks the knife left when it entered the body. In some stabbings, it's possible for the tip of the knife to break off, and this is just one clue that helps a ME (medical examiner) identify what kind of weapon was used in the stabbing.

Since knives vary, a medical examiner can often determine the length and type of blade used by analyzing the wound, so if your victim is stabbed, be sure the knife you've chosen suits the crime.

The skin edges of a stab wound are called the wound's margins, and the ends (or tips) are the wound's angles. Wounds are measured from one angle to the other.

Double-edge blades usually leave pointed, clean-cut edges and no bruising. Blunt objects, like scissors, tend to bruise and scrape the wound margin. The blunter the object is, the more often the entry hole is ragged and split.

Some things an ME looks for when analyzing are pattern, size, and borders of the wound, the motion used, how forceful the murderer was during the attack, sharpness/dullness of tip, the tissue encountered, and whether there are any visible defensive wounds. This analysis helps determine the object that was used on the victim.

<u>Typical characteristics of stab wounds</u>

- Kitchen knives have a pointed edge
- Stab wounds have clean edges
- Knives with blade guards sometimes leave unique bruising
- Serrated knives leave serrations
- Wounds created with something other than a knife sometimes leave noteworthy patterns (like the X on a Phillips-head screwdriver)
- Some screwdrivers and chisels will leave rectangular woundsIf a lot of force was used during the stabbing, bruising might be seen on the skin's surface because of the attacker's hand being in a fisted position while delivering blows
- When stabbing with scissors, the scissors can be open or closed. Open scissors leave distance between the wounds, whereas closed scissors have a noticeable Z shape

Poison

When I think of poison, I'm reminded of the movie *Arsenic and Old*

Lace with Cary Grant. It's one of my favorite black-and-white movies. The movie is about two old ladies who rent some of the rooms in their house to elderly bachelors. In the movie, the women poison the men with arsenic, justifying their murders with the notion that they're doing the old, lonely men a favor by murdering them.

One of the best examples of a writer who used poison often and well in her books is Dame Agatha Christie who was said to have used poison as the method of murder more than any other crime writer. Of her sixty-six mysteries, poison was the method of murder in about half of her stories.

If you want to learn about how to include poison as the murder weapon in your books, I'd suggest checking out a handful of her books: *Cards on the Table*, *Sparkling Cyanide*, and *The Crooked House*, to name a few.

What I like best about using poison in fiction is that poison is found in so many things. In many cases it's accessible, and depending on the poison used, sometimes it's still hard to discover.

In real life, female killers are known to poison more often than men, because it's simpler and easier, whereas men are often stronger and kill with much more force via gun, knife, strangling, etc.

The number one thing to consider when poisoning your victim is to make sure the poison you use matches the timeline of the victim's death.

Maybe you want your victim to survive the poisoning. In this scenario, you also need to ensure the poison you use is one where the victim's survival is possible.

Before I pick my poison, I always consider the method of death, and I ask myself these questions:

- How soon do I want the victim to die after being poisoned?

- How traceable do I want the poison to be (how easy is it for the ME to discover?)
- What kind of access does the murderer have to the poison?
- How much does the murderer need to know about the poison?
- How will the poison be administered?

Think outside the box when it comes to poisons. There are so many ways to poison a person from a snake bite, to poisonous plants, to downing a bottle of pills, rat poison, and even Calabar beans … the list of options is endless!

CHAPTER 18

"F" Is for Forensics

I've always been fascinated with forensics, and I have watched just about every episode of *Forensic Files*, which you can currently stream on Netflix. If you're just dipping a toe into the forensics world, I highly recommend binge-watching the series versus learning about forensics from fictional television shows that are often unrealistic.

Forensic Files covers actual cases and takes you through the process of how forensics was used to catch the killer.

I'd also suggest you read D.P. Lyle's book *Forensics for Dummies*, which he updated in 2019.

Moving on …

There are two types of crime scenes—primary and secondary.

A **primary scene** is the place the death occurred.

The **secondary scene** is the other location (or locations) where physical evidence is collected.

For example, let's say a woman is running through the forest, fleeing from her attacker. As she runs, she loses a shoe, an earring, and an article of clothing. These secondary items are gathered by investigators as they search for the body itself, in the primary scene where the murder took place.

Max Cady, who's crazy with a capital C, has just been murdered. Now he enters the stages of death:

- Pallor mortis
- Algor mortis
- Rigor mortis
- Cadaveric spasm
- Lividity
- Putrefaction
- Decomposition
- Skeletonization

<u>The three phases of mortis:</u>

1. **Pallor mortis** is the change in the victim's color. When a

person dies, the usual reddish tone we all have changes to blue, then gray, then white as the body decomposes. This is the first stage of death and begins when blood no longer circulates through the body. It occurs shortly after death.

2. **Algor mortis** relates to the change in body temperature, the cooling process after death. On average, humans are 98.6 degrees Fahrenheit, but the body temp will vary depending on the environment the body is in.

   Other factors also include air flow, how much clothing the person is wearing, and the overall size of the person. The average body loses one degree per hour.

3. **Rigor mortis** is when the body stiffens. The energy source in the body is gone, and without that, the body enters a rigid state, because the muscles contract and are tense.

   Right at death, the body is flaccid and limp. The conditions surrounding the body, including the temperature the person is in at the time of death, determines how fast things change.

   Muscles usually begin to stiffen one to two hours after death. This is first noticed in the eyelids, mouth, neck, and jaw. Limbs and other extremities are affected next between four to eight hours after death.

   Once the body is completely stiff (after approximately twelve hours when blood is no longer coursing through the system), the body will go through a process of relaxation again.

Before the murder victim is removed from the crime scene, he/she will almost always be examined on-site by a forensics expert (coroner, medical examiner, pathologist, etc.).

<u>These experts will usually have the following items on hand</u>:

- Apron (usually waterproof)
- Disposable gloves
- Thermometer
- Syringe
- Needles
- Formalin sample jars
- Sterile swabs for blood and fluid
- Pen, pencil, and other writing tools
- Plastic bags/envelopes
- Things to cover their hair and face
- Cutting needles and twine
- Autopsy dissection kit
- Tape recorder
- Flashlight
- Camera

Documentation taken at the crime scene involves photos, videos, sketches, and note-taking. Because it's a homicide, latent prints and trace evidence will be noted and collected as well.

Notes will be taken by a member of the crime scene team and will include the who, what, why, when, and how of the incident—at least what is known at that point. The date and time will be documented, along with who is present at the scene. Weather conditions will also be noted.

Any evidence that's collected for processing such as ash trays, cigarette butts, clothing, weapons, etc. is also recorded.

The description of the victim is documented, including the position the victim was in when he/she was found, what they were wearing, and whether any items are noticeably missing (such as, there is a bra but no shirt).

Recording the scene has been a lot more common in recent years because it gives a more dimensional view of the overall crime scene, and these notes are often admissible in court as evidence.

Photographing the crime scene is vital to the investigation because it shows the exact condition of the scene after it's discovered.

Investigators can refer back to the photos later on to reanalyze things they feel are relevant to the case. The body and the scene will be photographed before anything is moved or removed.

<u>When inspecting the victim's body, clothing, and surroundings, the following is assessed:</u>

1. Are there any signs of a struggle?
2. What type of clothing is the victim wearing?
3. Does the clothing fit the season of the year? If not, why?
4. What kind of jewelry is the victim wearing, if any? (style, color, type, ears pierced or not, wedding ring or not)
5. Does the clothing fit the victim? (Sometimes the body swells after death which may make the clothing appear like it doesn't fit right).
6. Does it appear the victim may have been undressed/redressed?
7. Is the victim clean or dirty?
8. What do the nails look like? (clean and trimmed, long, dirty, etc.)

9.   Is the clothing on the way it should be (buttons fastened, zippers zipped)?
10. If the victim is found in a home or other inside area, were the lights on or off when the victim was found?
11. Were there any mail or newspapers delivered that haven't been collected for a certain amount of time?
12.   Is there any food out or sitting in a sink that looks like it has been there for a while?
13. Does the victim have anything in his/her purse, car, pockets, etc. to establish something they were doing before they died?
14. Was anything left cooking, any appliances on?

<u>Some of the main items of note to be collected at a crime scene are:</u>

- Blood (scraped into a dry container or with a wet swab)
- Glass
- Weapons
- Soil
- Fingerprints (lifted from windows and doors, collected from smaller items)
- Blood spatter (photographed for distance/angle)
- Semen
- Hair/fibers
- Important documents
- Tire marks and footprints (measured, casts made, photos taken)
- Food/beverage
- Cigarette butts
- Pills

- If a sexual assault is suspected, a sexual battery kit will be used before the body is cleaned
- If there are signs of a struggle, scalp hair and fingernail scrapings and clippings will be taken

Everything collected will be labeled with a case number, time, and date, along with what was collected and who collected it.

After all the evidence is gathered, it's time for the victim to be transferred to the lab for further analysis. The body is placed into a body bag that zips up or on a plastic sheet. Sheets are wrapped over the body and secured so all physical evidence remains intact.

<u>When the body arrives at the coroner or medical examiner's lab, these professionals assess the body to determine the following:</u>

- The identity of the victim.
- How the victim died.
- When the victim died.
- Where the victim died.
- What caused their death.

Most coroners will start at the top of the head and move down as they complete their assessment, so the chances that they miss something is lessened. The body will be face up, and it will be searched for any unusual marks, bruises, or abrasions.

One of the things a coroner tries to determine first is whether the murder took place at the place where the body was found, or whether there's evidence to suggest there was a "body dump," indicating the victim was killed in one place and left at another.

Recommended Reads

Autopsies, Geoff Symon

Howdunit Forensics: A Guide for Writers, D.P. Lyle

Forensics: What Bugs, Burns, Prints, DNA, and More Tell Us About Crime, Val McDermid

CHAPTER 19

FACT OR FICTION: GETTING YOUR FACTS STRAIGHT

There is nothing worse than getting an email from a reader who is an expert on a topic you're writing about in your book, and they're reaching out to tell you about a blunder you've made. You're bound to get the occasional blowback from a reader who gets their thrills from letting you know when you've done something wrong. It's irritating and often times petty, but it happens. But when it's something you could have researched on your own, and didn't for whatever reason, it hurts even more. Ouch!

In other genres, such as a fantasy book about a fictitious world where witches and warlocks roam, no one can question what is or isn't possible because it's all make-believe. In mystery and suspense, some of what we write is based on reality, and every effort should be made to assure it is as accurate as possible.

Readers must believe that the story you present is plausible, something that could happen in real life. You can bend reality, but the story still needs to be believable. Writers of historical mysteries need to make sure everything about the setting is true to the time the story is set in. They also need to make sure the dialogue between characters includes words that were actually spoken in the time the book is set in.

I rarely receive complaint emails, but they do happen. As I sit here thinking about it, only two of significance come to mind. A lady emailed me once to say that the expensive bottle of wine I used in a story should not have been chilled in the honeymoon scene. She was right, and I felt like an idiot because not only do I research everything, my OCD dictates I over-research, so I ended up having a "how the hell did that happen" moment. If you *think* you know something, but you're not 100% sure, you better look it up.

If you delve into forensics and start throwing around words like lividity, livor mortis, and putrefaction, you better know how each one relates to the crime scene. At the very least you should know how things work, what happens when someone is murdered, how the time of death is determined, and what happens from that point on in a developing investigation.

Getting the details of the crime right is important, but other things are important too. I'm talking about the small things. When I'm writing a story that's based in a city or town I'm unfamiliar with, I spend time getting to know the place I'm writing about. Part of this is for myself. It gives me a visual that inspires me to include factual tidbits of information so the location comes alive when I write about it. I also look up the population size, the average wage, the average household size, the surrounding towns and cities, what county the city or town is in, etc. I like to scroll through a few pages of photos of the town or city as well, so I know how it looks in the season I've set the book in.

Readers get excited when you write a story about a place they live in, lived in, or have visited. The last thing you want is for them to be disappointed because you didn't capture the magic or ambiance of what it's like to actually have been there.

You also always want to look up the police station/department in the town or city to learn what it's called, the chain of command, and what the different titles/roles are. For example, in Las Vegas, they're called The Las Vegas Metropolitan Police Department or LVMPD for short. It is headed by a sheriff who's elected by the public every four years. In the New York City Police Department, they're known as the NYPD. They're overseen by a police commissioner who has been appointed by the mayor. Knowing these details makes a difference.

If you're doing forensics research seek out an expert in the area you're trying to learn about. I love D.P. Lyle's *Forensics and Fiction* and *More Forensics and Fiction* books (which should be in every suspense writer's library). He groups themes together and then answers many of the author questions he's received over the years. He's also worked with the writers of several popular television shows over the years and is considered to be an expert in the field of forensics. I'd also suggest checking out his blog, The Crime Fiction Writer's Blog and his cool podcast series Criminal Mischief: The Art & Science of Crime Fiction.

Another topic that's sensitive to readers is firearms. An article posted at the end of 2019 stated three in ten American adults own a gun themselves and another 11% live with someone who does. It's safe to assume that plenty of readers know a thing or two about firearms, and if you're going to use them in your books, you should be somewhat of an expert too.

The genre we write in provokes our readers to think, to form opinions, to agree or disagree with what we've said. Because of this, not only do we have the opportunity to make a lasting impression, we become teachers, and the readers become our students.

Whatever you write, do so with integrity. The pen or keyboard we use has the opportunity to wield mighty power. In one of my short stories, the issue of fentanyl-laced heroin, nicknamed "Killer Heroin" in the drug market, was a main theme of the story. At the end of the book, I included an afterword about the growing problem of Killer Heroin in today's society, and I shared a link for anyone who may be dealing with drug addiction themselves or know someone who is. It means a lot to me when I have the chance to shed light on things like this.

"As writers, we need to strip away our own ideals and slip inside the shoes of our readers."

As writers, we need to understand the difference between facts and opinions and respect that our readers won't always share the same views about things. Take pro-life and pro-choice for example. Most people have an opinion about it one way or the other. It doesn't mean one has been proven right and the other is wrong. It means one person may see it one way and others may see it another way. That's okay. It's also okay to include either in your book. What's *not* okay is when your readers think you're trying to *tell them* how they should feel instead of respecting differences of opinion. I guess what I'm saying is, as writers, we need to strip away our own ideals and slip inside the shoes of our readers. They'll appreciate you for being objective. Trust me on that.

CHAPTER 20

MUSIC & LYRICS: COPYRIGHT LAWS

I once read about a guy who included a bunch of one-liner song lyrics from different popular bands in his novel. He was sued by just about every single one of them for copyright infringement and given hefty fines. His book was stripped from bookshelves. Oops.

Now let's discuss what is okay and what isn't.

Lyrics are intellectual property, which means you don't have the right to use them without permission. Let me translate that for you … don't do it!

I've heard writers say things like, "Unless my book sells a ton of copies, who's going to know?"

Back when I was still green behind the ears in the book business, one of the characters in my books said a man reminded her of a famous actor (whom I named). A few months after the book's release, he followed me on social media, which was, well … cool, actually, but I'll be honest: it freaked me out to discover he'd heard about the mention I'd made of him in my book. Small world, right?

My point is, it's a lot easier for things to get out than you think, and when it comes to lyrics, those who own the rights are fiercely protective. Trust me when I say, without permission, it's never worth the risk.

Any song written or produced in the United States after 1924 requires permission from the creator, period, as all of the works after that time are copyrighted. Before 1924, a lot of music is part of public domain, but you'll still want to check to make 100% sure.

If there is a certain song you're wondering about, you can search for it on Copyright.gov, and then after you find out who owns the rights, you'll need to ask for permission *before* you include it in your novel.

Personally, I don't mess with this in my own writing. If I want my readers to know the song my character is whistling, I just include the title because the titles of books and songs aren't subject to copyright. I've also created my own lyrics before, and that can be a lot of fun.

If you've read everything I've just said and you're still interested in using something that's copyrighted, let's talk about how to acquire permission. First, try searching Google for the name of the publisher of the song you'd like to use. If you still can't figure out who it is, there are two main publishers you can query who represent thousands of artists: Hal Leonard Corporation and Alfred Music Publishing.

I just Googled: *Who is Nina Simone's publisher?* I discovered her rights have been acquired by BMG. I then searched *BMG Music* and found their website in about five seconds, so for most songs, a little research will point you in the right direction.

Before you send in your request, you must be prepared to provide them with the following:

- Publication title of your book
- Publication date of your book
- Exact lyrics you want to use in the publication
- Territory of distribution (all countries where your book will be sold)

- Number of copies you expect to be printed/sold (I'd go higher than lower)
- Suggested retail price of your book in all formats

Make sure you wait for their response <u>before</u> using the lyrics. Don't use it and assume you sent a message about your intentions and that's probably good enough, because it isn't.

For more information, check out this terrific article by Jane Friedman, A Writer's Guide to Fair Use and Permissions + Sample Permissions Letter.

One more small tidbit before I wrap up this section. Many authors are confused about how to write a song title, movie title, book name, etc. so I wanted to go over when to use quotations and when to use italics.

<u>When to use quotation marks:</u>
Song: "Four Women"
Short story: "Dead of Night"
Poem: "Dusty Ford Ranger"
Episode of a TV Show: "The One That Got Away"
Magazine/newspaper Article: "Cheryl's Tips for Cooking the Perfect Egg"

<u>When to use italics:</u>
Book: *Little Girl Lost*
Movie: *Stranger in Town*
TV show: *The Brokenwood Mysteries*
Magazine: *Psychology Today*
Newspaper: *the New York Times*
Album: *Long Road Home*

PART
TWO:
SELL IT

CHAPTER 21
TO AGENT OR NOT TO AGENT: THAT IS THE QUESTION

Over the years, several authors have asked me whether or not I have an agent and whether I thought they should get one. It's a hard question to answer because no two writing journeys are the same.

My first question to anyone considering being represented by an agent or seeking out one is always: why do you want one?

The answer I hear most is: "If I get an agent, I think I'll have a better chance of being published by a traditional publisher."

If that's important to you, and if it's a goal or dream you have, an agent may be of some benefit to you.

On the other hand, if you're wondering if you need an agent in order to publish and be successful … no, you don't.

I'm not 100% against having an agent. I've been represented in the past, and for me, I have learned an agent can be beneficial when it comes to negotiating foreign contracts, TV/movie deals, or large traditional book deals, which we don't see a lot of nowadays.

Once you have a few books out, you'll start getting an idea of how they sell and what you can expect to earn per book (gross and net). I highly recommend tracking your sales so you can measure them over time. That way you'll get an overall average of what the next book will be worth before it's even released. It's valuable information to have because if you decide to sign with an agent and you're offered a book deal, you'll already know whether or not to accept it.

Author Hercule Poirot was just offered a $20,000 advance for book one in his new series. The publisher is asking for a seven-year commitment, meaning the publisher owns the rights for those seven years. The publisher expresses an interest in giving him a contract for book two in the series as well, once it comes out, but for right now, they're only committed to signing him for book one.

Why?

Because they want to see how book one does before making an offer on any others.

The first thing I'd consider here is the fact that if Hercule's subsequent books aren't picked up by the publisher, and he wants to continue writing the series, any book he publishes will keep selling the first book; more often than not, readers like to read a series in its entirety, even if the books could be read as a stand-alone novel.

Let's go back to the advance for a minute. In most cases, Hercule will have to earn out the $20k he's been given *before* he starts receiving any royalty checks. Unless the book is heavily promoted and does well, that's going to take a while because the publisher and the agent (if he has one) will take their percentage of the royalty first and then what's left goes to the author. On a $5 eBook, at 70% royalty, the publisher gets around $3.50. Of that, the publisher gives him 15%, and of the 15%, 20% goes to the agent. That $20k is not looking so great now, is it?

But money isn't the only thing to consider. The publisher's plans and promises they make to promote the book also matter. If they've committed to spend a hefty amount to promote it and give the book its best chance at succeeding, that's another thing to take into consideration. And now I have Janet Jackson's song "What Have You Done For Me Lately" stuck in my head.

One other consideration is time. We all know time is money, and I don't want to finish a book, sign with a traditional publisher, and wait a year or more for them to publish the book, so turnaround time matters too. Some publishers are faster than others. Every day that book isn't up for sale, Hercule loses money, and he knows exactly how much he's losing because he knows how much each of his books makes when it's released.

A lot of new authors think if they sign with a traditional publisher, the publisher is going to do all sorts of things for them to promote the book when it comes out. Sometimes they do, but a more likely scenario if you want the book to do well is to understand you'll need to work hard on your end as well.

Let's say you have an agent and you've signed with a traditional publisher for a three-book deal. The contract states the publishing house holds the rights to those books for ten years. You put book one out; it sells well for a while, but then it loses steam. Book two comes out, and it doesn't sell as well as book one did. The same thing happens for book three.

What do you think the publisher is likely to do?

If you're thinking they might stop promoting those three books, you're right, and because they hold the rights for a number of years, there's nothing you can do in most cases except wait it out or see if you can buy your way out of the contract.

On the flip side, I've known authors whose first traditionally published book had great sales, and the publisher went on to sign the next two books in the series, promoted them well, and nice profits were made all the way around. The business we're in comes with risks. Some pay off, some don't.

I also know an author whose first traditionally published novel was a huge success. It sold so well the book was made into a movie starring A-List actors. She wrote several other novels after, and they were all signed different publishing houses. None of those books sold as well as her first one did. And her last book, which came out about a year ago, only has four reviews. In this business, it's hard to predict what will happen.

"Over the years I've learned what matters most is to focus on building my brand and to keep investing in myself."

I've been in the eleventh hour of signing a contract and have had the bottom fall out right at the end for one reason or another. It's a fickle business. You never know what's going to happen. I've also had books that were passed on by traditional publishers that went on to make the *USA Today* Best-Selling Books list. Over the years I've learned what matters most is to focus on building my brand and to keep investing in myself.

If you're still interested in getting an agent and trying to sign with one of the main publishing houses, the four big houses are:

Penguin/Random House/Simon and Schuster

Hachette Book Group

Harper Collins

Macmillan

Before you approach them, you'll need to get an agent. You can do that by heading over to AALA Association of American Literary

Agents. Here you can search by genre, click on the agents you're interested in and see if they're accepting submissions.

If you submit a query, make sure you follow the instructions *perfectly*. I've talked to plenty of agents who have said that when they receive queries that aren't <u>exactly</u> what they asked for, they pass on the query without even reading it because the instructions weren't followed. Take your time, look your submission over, and do give them what they ask for—nothing more, nothing less.

CHAPTER 22

TIES THAT BIND: SERIES VS. STAND-ALONE

I remember reading my first Robert B. Parker book a couple of decades ago and falling in love with his Spenser series. From that point on, I read every single book in that series and then moved on to his two other series and read those as well.

Parker was once asked how long he would continue his main series, and he said he'd keep at it as long as fans kept reading it. And he did just that. Spenser books were written right up to the time Parker passed away in 2010. Since then, his Spenser, Sunny Randall, and Jesse Stone series have continued on with other authors at the helm. Ace Atkins writes the Spenser series, and Mike Lupica writes Sunny Randall and Jesse Stone.

What can we learn from this?

Readers love falling in love with a character and everyone involved in that character's world. Give your reader a character they clamor for, and you'll strike gold. Readers will be counting down the days until the next book in the series comes out.

"Have you ever watched a TV series you didn't want to end? Readers feel the same way when they become hooked."

I have written both series and stand-alone books, and in my experience, even though all four stand-alone novels have been profitable, they're nowhere near as profitable as my series books. If I could rewind the clock, I would take those stories and make them part of one of my main series instead. There was no way for me to know that until I tried, however, and your experience could be a lot different than mine.

When readers finish one of your books and they like it, they become invested. They can't wait for more. Think of it this way: have you ever watched a TV series you didn't want to end? Of course, you have. For me, the show *Penny Dreadful* is one of the first that comes to mind. I could have binge-watched it forever (so maybe it's a good thing that it ended when it did). You get the idea of what I'm saying though, and your readers feel the same when they become hooked on one of your books.

Let's take readers out of the equation for a minute and talk about something else ... money. Writing a series affords you a lot of amazing opportunities.

Let's say you've written four books in a series. You now have enough books to really start experimenting.

<u>A few experiments I've tried:</u>

1. Discounting the first book in the series by 50%.

I'm not a big fan of making the first book free unless it's for a short-term BookBub ad or some other highly visible promo. I've found charging $2.99 for the first books works just fine for our genre, and that most readers still see $2.99 as a good discount.

I will say others have made their first book free, and they swear by it, especially romance authors. But on average, our books sell at a slightly higher price point.

2.   Discounting the third book out of four.

It may sound strange, but there's a method to my madness. When you discount the third book and you have two books before it and one after it in the series, it gives a sales boost to the other books because you'll have a percentage of readers who will want to purchase the other books too. When I do this, I keep the other books at full price.

If I apply for a BookBub ad using a book from my established series, I usually skip the first couple of books in the series and choose books four to six. I love choosing the books in the middle because I always make money on the books that come before and after the discounted book.

3.   Creating a side series using main series characters.

Why not give your popular character a side hustle? This idea is a great one to try once you've written at least four books in the series and have a decent following of readers invested in the characters of that series.

I took the characters from my Sloane Monroe series and created a spinoff series called "Sloane Monroe Stories." They are shorter works (most between 15 to 20k words). The theme of each book is one of the seven deadly sins, and each book involves Sloane and one other secondary character from the main series.

I do almost nothing to promote the novella series but because the books are priced at $1.99, $2.99, and $3.99 (a price I base on each book's individual length), they seem to get enough visibility on their own.

What's great about this is that I can write these shorter works quickly, and I still make a decent profit on them. This has been one of the most successful ideas I've tried to date when it comes to books I do almost nothing to promote.

CHAPTER 23

GOING ALL IN:
WIDE VS. KDP SELECT

Everyone has their own unique experience when it comes to making books exclusive on KDP Select as opposed to "going wide," where your books are available at as many retailers as possible. In a nutshell, it's not a "one size fits all" situation where I can tell you whether you should be exclusive with Amazon or not, but I will go over them both.

If you're on the fence or thinking about going all in with KDP Select and having your books in Kindle Unlimited, my suggestion would be to try KDP Select for a few months and then put your books on Amazon as well as other retailers for a few months (going wide) and then compare the two.

I know I've said this several times in this book, but I'll always support each individual author in doing what works best for them personally. I've seen other authors try to model themselves and their brand around other authors they admire. There's nothing wrong with learning from other authors and then trying to level up. I highly recommend it, in fact. But if something isn't working for you after you've worked at it for a while, don't feel like you need to keep throwing away your money and/or time if it's not working.

In this business, you could very easily try and fail 50 times, and then the 51st time you find something that works well. The difference is in taking the time to tweak and rework things until you know you've done all you can and then let it go if it isn't working.

Back in the early days of Amazon when books could be opted into KDP Select, I made my main series exclusive, and I became really good at knowing which tips and tricks to use to keep my books trending at a lower ranking in the Kindle Store.

Everything changed with the introduction of KDP Select's Kindle Unlimited program a couple of years later, when authors started being paid for pages read instead of a fixed price when a book was borrowed. Everything I'd been doing successfully no longer worked, and I struggled to figure out how to use it to my advantage. I decided it was a good time to go wide and expand my fan base as much as I could on other platforms, and I'm glad I did.

At the moment, I make more money keeping my Sloane Monroe series wide than having the books exclusive on Amazon's platform. This is due to a few factors. First, I've spent the last eight years selling on the other platforms, and I have built up a readership outside of Amazon. Don't get me wrong here. Amazon still gives me the lion's share, but the others add up enough to keep me interested in staying wide. And second, traditionally published authors have started putting their books into KDP Select, and I believe this has made it much harder to get visibility in the program.

My Addison Lockhart series is a bit different. It's a ghost/supernatural mystery series, and every time I make it exclusive on Amazon for a few months, it does better than my Sloane Monroe series does in there. I may not know the exact reason why, but I have a theory. Niche genres tend to do better in the program in subgenres where there is better visibility because there are less books in them. Because of this, I'll write more book series like this in the future.

<u>The major retailers where you can publish your book are:</u>

Amazon KDP

Barnes and Noble Press

Kobo Writing Life

Apple Books

Google Play Books

<u>If you're going wide (not exclusive with Amazon), you have two options:</u>

1. You can create an account on each individual platform yourself.

2. You can upload your book to Draft2Digital or Smashwords, and they'll do it for you in exchange for a small percentage of the profits. Both take 10% percent of the retail price (15% net).

<u>Draft2Digital currently publishes to the following vendors:</u>
- Amazon
- Apple Books
- Barnes & Noble

- Kobo (including Kobo Plus)
- Tolino
- OverDrive
- Bibliotheca
- Scribd
- 24Symbols
- Baker & Taylor
- Hoopla
- Vivlio

<u>Smashwords currently publishes to the following vendors:</u>

- Apple Books
- Smashwords
- Barnes & NobleKobo
- Scribd
- Tolino
- Overdrive
- Bibliotheca
- Odilo
- Gardners
- Califa
- Fnac
- Askews & Holts
- Browns Books for Students
- Baker & Taylor
- Livraria Cultura
- Hive
- Axis 360
- Blio

Both Draft2Digital and Smashwords are great people to work with. I personally use Draft2Digital. I love the platform, they're always quick to respond to my questions, and they're just terrific people all around.

I publish to Amazon, Barnes & Noble, Kobo, and Google Play Books myself and use Draft2Digital for all other vendors. I also like D2D because of all of the wonderful value-added services they offer, like creating a single, personalized link to your books on all vendors through Books2Read and the ability to create paperback books.

CHAPTER 24

IT'S A WRAP:
QUALITY BOOK COVERS

Before a reader even gets to a book's blurb, they see the book's cover. If they don't connect to it, you can (and should) expect them to keep on scrolling. And unless you possess super-ninja book graphic design skills, you'll need to hire a professional designer to work on the book cover for you.

Cover designers can vary greatly in price, depending on skill level and type of book cover. The fee could be anywhere from one hundred dollars or less for a pre-made cover (a cover that's already made and just needs your name and title added to it), and up to several hundreds of dollars for an artist who will build you a layered cover from scratch.

<u>When considering the cover for your story, make sure:</u>
- The cover relates to the genre
- The cover graphic ties into the story somehow

"When you're working on a cover with your designer, try to think like a reader, and remember, this is your first opportunity to sell your book."

If you don't know where to start, I suggest scrolling through Amazon's mystery, thriller, and suspense pages for ideas. I'm not suggesting you copy another author's cover. Please don't. I'm just suggesting it's a great way to find examples of what the covers of successful books look like and what themes are trending in our genre at the moment.

I was just scrolling through the top-100 list in Mystery, and I noticed over half the books have covers depicting outdoor scenery (house, cottage, cabin, water, snow, ice, woods, field, flower, rain clouds, ocean, lake). 34 of the 100 include a person on the cover. And shades of blue/green/red seem popular right now.

When you're working on a cover with your designer, try to think like a reader, and remember, this is your first opportunity to sell your book.

<u>Book Covers should:</u>

- Be easy to understand/interpret (not confusing)
- Have titles and subtitles that are clear
- Have a main focal point
- Entice the reader to read the book's description
- Give an idea of what the book is about

- Be designed to target your core audience
- Make your reader feel something
- Be bold/clear as a sample/thumbnail size (the one most vendors use)

What about taglines? Add? Don't Add? Do they even matter?

Sometimes they add to the cover. Other times they take away (especially if they're too long). Either way, they should be short, to the point, not take up too much space, and leave the reader wanting more.

In that top 100 Mystery, Thriller & Suspense list I was just referring to, only five books had taglines. I've listed three great examples below, and somehow, the titles all ended up being three words long, *and* all start with "The." Spooky. Perhaps "the" is another new trend I've stumbled upon.

This trio of books offers perfect examples of how to do a tagline right:

The Guest List

The Other Wife

The Silent Wife

Sidebar: As for these all being three-word titles, books in our genre tend to have shorter titles. Only 22 titles in the top-100 list at the time of this writing are over three words long. Just something to consider.

We've discussed the front of the book, but what about the back of your paperback?

Keep it clean and uncluttered, much like the front, but include a few important items like:

- Your name
- A recent photo of yourself
- Your book's description, or a condensed version if it's long
- Social proof (one or two short accolades taken from reviews, fellow authors, book reviewers, etc.) who have read and reviewed your book.

Here's an example of the layout of my paperback book *Eye for Revenge*, and I'd suggest scrolling through the Mystery/Thriller pages on Amazon to get other ideas too.

Now, let's shift gears and look at some eBook cover ideas and talk about what works, what doesn't work, and why.

Black Diamond Death was the first book I wrote and published, and as you can see, it's had a few different covers. Keep in mind, I was very new and unexperienced back then, so it took me some time to get it right.

The first cover had a tagline that said: *Sometimes accidents aren't what they seem.* It's a good tagline, but I'm sure it could have been even better. Even now, I still think the cover is cute, but a cartoonish look is better for cozies, and this isn't a cozy mystery.

Version 2 looked more like a mystery, but I didn't like that the title wasn't clear, and the graphic was also a single image, and I prefer layered images, so I don't see another author with the same exact cover graphic as the one I'm using. This one was all right, but I still thought it could be better, so I had it redone once more.

Version 3 is the cover that I'm using today, and I like how it came out. It generates questions and intrigue the other two lacked. Even so, I will probably change it again sometime!

Sinnerman was the second book I wrote and published, and I still love the cover and the title of the book. BUT. This is a good example of being crazy about something that doesn't quite fit with the demographic you're targeting. And since you've just read my tips on creating a great book cover, when you look at version 1, what do *you* think is wrong?

Let's start with the title.

With *Sinnerman*, I was paying homage to the late, great singer Nina Simone. But not everyone knows the song or knows the singer. The title font is also cool, but it's hard to read, and my name is practically nonexistent.

In Version 2, I changed the title of the book to *Murder in Mind*. This is something I suggest not doing unless you really need to do it because it can cause confusion with your readers. In this case, I knew I needed to do it.

At this point, I'd found a title font I liked, which I now use on all my books in the Sloane Monroe series today. But I didn't like this cover. I didn't think it was ominous enough, for starters, and something about that coffee cup the girl is holding drove me crazy.

Plus, placing the victim in a park in the daytime is never as off-putting as a park at night.

Version 3 was created by a different cover designer. This time it came out how I had always imagined it could.

I Have a Secret is the third book I wrote, and you can see a big difference between these covers and the earlier versions of the other two books in this series. I actually like all three of covers, but again, day isn't always as menacing as night. I used cover two for several years and just changed it out a couple months ago with Version 3.

Why?

To breathe new life back into an older backlist title from 2013 and to capture more of the demographic I may have missed with the previous cover. Maybe they saw it. Maybe they liked it. But they didn't like it enough to buy it. A new cover may change their mind.

Put It to the Test

Another idea is to test out a few covers *before* the book goes on sale to see which cover generates the most interest. The easiest way to do this is by creating targeted Facebook ads so you can determine which one a reader finds the most appealing.

Many of Stephen King's books have gone through cover revisions over the years. *IT* has had over a dozen.

Looking for a cover designer who will create something from scratch? I've listed several below, including Reedsy, which is like one-stop shopping where you can browse through their lists of designers and then request a quote.

Good Cover Design

Book Covers Art

Rocking Book Covers

Reedsy

100 Covers

Killion Publishing

Cathy's Covers

And here are a few great sites to check out for cheaper pre-made book covers:

Go On Write

Paper & Sage

Self-Pub Book Covers

Indie Designz

Rocking Book Covers

Book Cover Zone

Studioenp

CHAPTER 25

WHAT'S THE WORD:
BOOK BLURBS

Once a reader becomes intrigued by your spectacular book cover, they'll move on to the book's description and then hopefully buy the book. The book description is your sales pitch. It's the first opportunity a reader has to get to know the inside of the book as well as the outside.

> "We're living in a fast-paced society. A well-written paragraph or two, followed by a few accolades is all that's needed."

One thing I see all the time is book descriptions that are waaaaaaaay too long. It isn't necessary to write a full-page description, followed by thousands of accolades from readers who have read and reviewed the book. We're living in a fast-paced society. A well-written paragraph or two, followed by a few accolades is all that's needed.

It's not about length.

It's about the quality of the description itself.

And it's about the social proof that goes along with it.

<u>What is Social Proof?</u>

Social proof is when people mimic a certain behavior because others have done it. Remember when the "cronut" first became popular? People lined up outside the bakery's New York City location (Dominique Ansel Bakery) before the store even opened to get one. They waited an hour or more, which makes it an excellent example of social proof.

If *everyone else* thinks it's good, it must be … Right?

When you're browsing a book page, trying to decide whether you want to purchase the book, and in the review section you see one of your favorite authors endorsed the book you're considering, that's social proof.

It's "proof" on your book's page that suggests/influences the reader to download your book. Reviews by other readers or testimonials from other authors is one form of social proof in the book marketing world. Another form is the accolades the book or series may have received, such as hitting a bestseller list or winning an award.

<u>Your book's description should:</u>

- Hook the reader in the first line
- Introduce the protagonist
- Present the main conflict
- Reveal what's at stake
- Make the reader feel the book is for them
- Use words that evoke emotion

<u>Your book's description should not:</u>
- Be longer than it needs to be
- Be confusing (reader can't tell what the story is about)
- Contain spoilers
- Give false information/accolades that aren't factual

Now, let's check out a few examples of different types of effective book descriptions:

Example 1

2020 *USA Today* Bestselling Book.

Grace Ashby wakes to the sound of a horrifying scream.

She races down the hallway and finds her mother's lifeless body on the floor in a pool of blood. Her mother's boyfriend Hugh is hunched over her. At first glance it seems Hugh is to blame, but is Hugh really her mother's killer?

As revelations about Caroline Ashby's secret life unfold, private detective Sloane Monroe takes the case, but it won't take long to find the killer. He's been watching, carefully tracking her every move, and now Sloane's own life is in grave danger.

Readers of the Sloane Monroe Series are saying: *"While I've found most mystery/thrillers to be rehashes of the same old plot line, this was refreshingly new/original."*—Jack Murphy, New York Times bestselling author of *Reflexive Fire*

"Bradshaw writes a great thriller, with likeable characters, and a taunt timeline that keeps you reading way past lights-out."—Amazon Vine Voice Top 500 Reviewer

This is from my book *Smoke and Mirrors*, and I use a similar setup for all of my books. It took several years to get my descriptions exactly how I wanted them, but I really like this arrangement, and it works for me. It's also spaced out in a way that makes it easy to read and understand.

I include social proof at the top to let the reader know the book hit the USA Today list. For my books that don't hit a list, that top line is usually a short accolade from another author.

Then I go right into the story by mentioning the primary characters, the murder, and what's at stake. I also include a cliffhanger, by posing a question to suggest Hugh may or may not be the actual killer.

Example 2

The Missing...

In a hidden basement, eighteen-year-old Toni is held captive and no one can hear her screams. She's been abducted after investigating unspeakable things in the darkest corners of the Internet.

The Vigilante...

Fearing the worst, Toni's mother turns to ex-SAS operative Mitchell to help find her missing daughter. And when Mitchell discovers Toni's fate rests in the hands of pure evil, he races against the clock to find Toni and bring her out alive. But even that might not be enough to save her.

The Detective...

DS Warren Carter is looking forward to a new job and a simpler life. But when he's called in to investigate the brutal murder of a seemingly normal couple, he becomes entangled in lives that are anything but simple. And as he digs deeper, he uncovers a crime more twisted than he could ever have imagined.

Into the Darkness is the chilling new thriller from the bestselling author of *Duplicity* and *Beneath the Surface*.

This is from *Into the Darkness* by Sibel Hodge. I really like how she set this up by giving insight into three of the main characters of the book.

Below the description she adds a line of social proof. It's subtle and well-crafted, and it lets the reader know this book was written by a bestselling author.

Example 3

OVER 1,000,000 series copies sold

"Lawrence Kelter is an exciting new novelist, who reminds me of an early Robert Ludlum.

—Nelson DeMille

"Kelter is a master, pure and simple."
—The Kindle Book Review

"Chalice's acerbic repartee is like an arsenal of nuclear missiles."
—BookWire Review

NYPD's street savvy detective Stephanie Chalice is back and not a minute too soon. Her newest nemesis is a con artist and bloodthirsty killer, a chameleon able to change her identity at will, a ghost known only as Black. Chalice is called into action when a billionaire's ward, an autistic child, is abducted from beneath the nose of his well-trained bodyguard. Black's reason for choosing this mark is not the obvious one. The kidnap victim is no ordinary child; he has never learned to read or write, and yet is capable of channeling the prophecies of his long dead ancestor; those that have long been memorialized, and those now thought to be ages lost. Chalice is put to the test, forced to decipher clues that defy explanation. Will she be able to outthink her diabolical opponent before it's too late?

This example is from *Ransom Beach* by Lawrence Kelter. I like the social proof at the top, which makes it clear this book has sold a lot of copies and is a popular book.

Below that is more social proof in the form of a few short accolades, and then he writes an excellent paragraph introducing the main character, the storyline, and the victim—a child a reader can easily invest in after reading a few sentences.

Example 4

A missing child sets the lives of three women on a collision course in this powerful and compelling novel by *USA Today* bestselling author Bette Lee Crosby.

1971.

When a music festival rolls through the sleepy town of Hesterville, Georgia, the Dixon family's lives are forever changed. On the final night, a storm muffles the sound of the blaring music, and Rachel tucks her baby into bed before falling into a deep sleep. So deep, she doesn't hear the kitchen door opening. When she and her husband wake up in the morning, the crib is empty. Emily is gone.

Vicki Robart is one of the thousands at the festival, but she's not feeling the music. She's feeling the emptiness over the loss of her own baby several months before. When she leaves the festival and is faced with an opportunity to fill that void, she is driven to an act of desperation that will forever bind the lives of three women.

When the truth of what actually happened that fateful night is finally exposed, shattering the lives they've built, will they be able to pick up the pieces to put their families back together again?

Winner of the Royal Palm Literary Award for Women's Fiction; the Readers' Favorite Gold Medal for Southern Fiction; and the FAPA President's Book Award for Women's Fiction.

This book description for *Emily, Gone* by Bette Lee Crosby reminds me of the sandwich rule. The opening line is fantastic. It combines an introduction to the character with social proof about Bette being a *USA Today* bestselling author. Sandwiched in the middle is a great description, followed by one more example of social proof, the three awards this book has won.

CHAPTER 26

CHA-CHING: PRICING YOUR EBOOK

Making money and getting your books in front of as many eyeballs as possible is exciting, but if you're at the beginning of your journey, I hope you understand it's going to take a lot of time before your hard work pays off. How much time it takes depends on several factors, including how fast you write, how much money you're putting back into your brand each month, and how quickly your fan base develops.

When I first started in 2011 there weren't as many authors publishing as there are today. It was the beginning of a new era wherein free and $0.99 books reigned supreme. You may have just read that sentence, shaken your head and thought there's no way you'd ever sell your work at such a low price point—because you've worked far too hard on your novel to give it away for chump change.

I understand your concerns, and now I'd like to offer you a different perspective.

Jan is shopping for a new mystery book at her favorite online book retailer. She finds one called *Ding Dong Dead*, and it looks intriguing. It's the first of several books in a series. The cover is impressive, and the blurb leaves her wanting more. She checks the price, and it's $4.99. That doesn't seem like a lot of money, right? But Jan has never read anything from the author of *Ding Dong Dead* before, and she's not sure she wants to pay $4.99 for a book she may not like.

Let's rewind and become Gwyneth Paltrow's character in the movie *Sliding Doors* for a minute.

Jan is shopping for a new mystery. She comes across *Ding Dong Dead*. It looks intriguing, the cover is impressive, the blurb leaves her wanting more, AND it's priced at $0.99. At such a great deal, she doesn't care that she's never heard of the author before. The $0.99 price is a low risk to take, and she takes it.

Jan reads *Ding Dong Dead* and loves it. She returns to her favorite book retailer to find the next book in the series. Book two is priced at $4.99. The difference now is that Jan has already been reeled in with book one. Now she's hooked. She loves the author's writing style. She loves the book's characters. She <u>must</u> have the next book, and she must have it now. It no longer matters to Jan that the next book costs more than the first one she read. She's become a fan of the author.

Instead of looking at price points in terms of how much money you're gaining or losing, look at it more in terms of how much a reader is worth over time. What you're interested in isn't just the here-and-now—you're interested in ten years from now and twenty years from now when Jan has read every book you've ever written. When you look at it from that perspective, that free or $0.99 first book in the series may not earn you the kind of money you deserve today, but in two years from now when you've published the fourth book in the series, I doubt you'll see it the same way.

It doesn't matter how many readers I have, how many social media followers I have, or how many people are signed up to my author newsletter. I am <u>always</u> trying to find new readers, and even though my name is known in the mystery world, there are still tons of readers out there who have never heard of me … *yet*.

When I first started, I priced book one in my series at $0.99, the second at $1.99, and the third at $2.99, and so forth. I priced like this for the first two or three years and then over time I raised it as my readership grew.

Here's how I structure pricing for my Sloane Monroe series today (unless I'm running a promotion on one, which I usually do for one of the books in the series each month):

Book 1: $2.99

Book 2: $4.99

Book 3: $4.99

Book 4: $4.99

Book 5: $5.99

Book 6: $5.99

Book 7: $5.99

Book 8: $5.99

I wouldn't suggest using these prices until you've been publishing for a while and have acquired a following, but once you're established, go for it.

<u>If I were a new author just starting out, I'd price the first four books like this:</u>

Book 1: Free

Book 2: $0.99

Book 3: $2.99

Book 4: $3.99

And this is specific to the genres we write in. Romance authors have enormous success making the first in their series free, but I find it's a bit of a different ballgame in the mystery/thriller market. Romance readers are younger and more rabid. They might read ten or more books in a week. We have older readers who are willing to pay more but don't always read as fast. When you're just starting out though, you'll want to price competitively until you have an established fan base.

CHAPTER 27

WORD UP:
AMAZON CATEGORIES & KEYWORDS

When you enter the details about your book on KDP Select, Amazon allows you to choose two categories for the book to be in. One thing I see authors do sometimes is put their book in categories it doesn't belong in. There is some crossover depending on the categories you choose, but not always. For example, let's say Hannibal Lecter decides to write a book and he puts it into the psychological thriller category. Great. Plausible. No problem.

As his second category, Hannibal chooses cozy mystery, because he thinks he can pull in potential readers who might be interested in his book because cozy *is* a subgenre of mystery. He also thinks the more eyes on his masterpiece, the better.

Hannibal is going about it all wrong and setting himself up for bad reviews from readers who think they're getting a cozy, and, instead, end up feeling ripped off.

Why?

Because cozies are books where violence and sex do not occur within the pages of the book, and Hannibal's book contains more violence than a gunfight at the O.K. Corral.

I'm all for branching out into subgenres that fit your story, but with so many great categories to choose from, there's no reason to market to an audience of readers who aren't your core demographic.

<u>A few tips when choosing your categories:</u>

Don't choose two of the same categories. For example, instead of choosing Mystery > Police Procedurals and Mystery > Private Investigator, choose one in Mystery, and the other in something like Thriller > Crime.

When you select your categories, don't choose mystery and thriller and be done with it. Drill down farther into something like Mystery > Hardboiled instead. Why? Because you'll get more visibility this way.

If you find you're interested in a category you saw on Amazon, but you don't see it listed on the product page when you're filling in the information about your book so you can publish it, go ahead and choose a second category for now, and then after you publish, you can send an email and request them to change it for you.

Example: Mystery > Series is a category in the Amazon store, but on the KDP book product page, it doesn't exist. Not today, anyway.

<u>How do you request a change?</u>

1. On the top of your Bookshelf page, highlighted in blue, is the word *Help*. Click on it.
2. Scroll down to the bottom of the page, and on the left side, click on the yellow tab that says: *Contact Us*.
3. In yellow, you will see: *How Can We Help?*

4. Choose *Amazon Product Page and Expanded Distribution.*
5. Choose *Update Amazon Categories.*

Once you get to this step, you'll see a text box for you to enter your information. This is what you want to say:

Hello,
I would like to request a category change for the book DING DONG DEAD by Mary Westmacott ASIN: B00MIH3NWU.

Please remove the category:
Mystery, Thriller & Suspense > Mystery > Cozy

And replace it with:
Mystery, Thriller & Suspense > Mystery > Series

Thank you,
Mary Westmacott

<u>Thinking outside the box</u>

There are so many categories in Mystery, Thriller & Suspense, sometimes writers don't consider trying other categories that may suit their book as well. I mentioned this at the start of this book, but now let's look at some great examples of other categories that sometimes cross over, depending on the theme of your book.

Looking at the current categories, some of my books (depending on the characters, series, and overall theme of the individual book) could fit in other categories such as:

- Lesbian, Gay, Bisexual & Transgender eBooks
     > Mystery & Detective

- Literature & Fiction
    > Horror

- Literature & Fiction
    > Anthologies & Literature Collections
    > Horror

- Literature & Fiction
    > Genre Fiction
    > Psychological

- Romance
    > Mystery & Suspense

- Teen & Young Adult
    > Mysteries & Thrillers

Hopefully this has given you an idea of how to branch out into other genres the right way with books that may suit other audiences outside of the main Mystery and Thriller categories.

Think about the themes in your book and then take a look at the categories and see what other categories might be worth exploring.

<u>How often should you change your book categories on Amazon?</u>

I don't believe there's a right or wrong answer here, but I've read articles where authors say they change their categories every few months and that they have seen a big difference when they do. I think it all comes down to how many books are in that category at that time. If it's a popular category with a ton of books and you weren't selling very many copies before the change, don't expect anything to be different without running promotions to boost visibility. Smaller subgenres are a better idea to try, and you're more likely to get noticed because you're competing with fewer books.

Sometimes Amazon will also add your book to additional categories if they feel your book is a good match. Short Stories is one subgenre I find them adding my books to sometimes. Books will be added to a category or subcategory that doesn't exist on the category list. This happened to one of my books recently, so I decided to see if they'd put some of my other shorter works into that category as well. They let me know it was a special category that couldn't be requested, which I found interesting.

If you're wondering what categories your books are in, you can find the categories on BKLNK.COM.

<u>Choosing effective keywords</u>

There's been a lot of discussion about how the right keywords can give your books the ability to stand out and get noticed. No one is a better expert on this subject than Dave Chesson and the awesome program he created called Publisher Rocket.

So … what is Publisher Rocket?

In short, the program shows you what keywords readers on Amazon are typing in and how many times those keywords are being searched each month. And that's just the beginning. Learn more about it at Publisher Rocket.

CHAPTER 28

HIT THE STREET: STARTING A STREET TEAM/ FAN CLUB

Once you have established yourself and you have subscribers to your newsletter and fans on your social media pages, it's time to build a street team, which is just a cool way of saying you're building a sweet fan club for your most rabid fans. A street team is a marketing term that describes a group of people who "hit the streets" to promote you and your wares.

I have two private street team groups on Facebook. One is for newbies who have either just been added or are on the newbie list because they're fans but not rabid fans. The other, my main group, is for my hardcore fans. Most of them have read everything I've written, and they're great about sharing the news and information about my books with their family and friends and on social media.

Over the years, some of my hardcore fans have become like family, and I love interacting with them. Before we get into more about that, I'd first like to show you how I went about getting readers involved in my street team in the first place.

<u>How do you find members and start a street team?</u>

I use my newsletter to find new members. It's the perfect place to get them from because that's where a lot of my most engaged readers are.

Once or twice a year, I send out a newsletter and the wording I use is similar to this:

Are You One of Cheryl Bradshaw's Biggest Fans?

Have you read all of her books?

Then You Should Join Her Street Team!

LET'S TALK ELIGIBILITY

Anyone is eligible to sign up. For this round, we'll be adding 30 new members to Cheryl's main street team. Everyone else will be added to the newbie team where there are still plenty of opportunities to take part in the fun.

LET'S TALK REWARDS

Members of Cheryl's team get perks like free books and prizes, which we award on a fun, points-based system. The prizes we give away include gift cards, mugs, signed books, T-shirts, and so much more!

LET'S TALK SIGNING UP

To sign up to become a member of Cheryl's exclusive street team, click on the link below and fill out the form. Whether you make the main list or are added to the newbie list, you'll receive an email from us letting you know.

Thank you for your interest in becoming part of her team!

I like to keep the newsletter short and sweet because nowadays most people don't have a long attention span.

Potential new street team members fill out a form I've created on Google Forms.

On the form I ask questions like:

What makes you one of Cheryl's biggest fans?
What is your favorite Cheryl Bradshaw book?

The reason why I ask is because I'm looking for true fans to add to the main group, and the questions help narrow down the best candidates.

You'd be surprised at how many people answer, "I don't know" or "I haven't read one of Cheryl's books yet, but I want to soon." These people are *potential* fans, but they don't belong on the main street team.

Once a reader is a member of the main street team, they are eligible to receive all of the books I put out from that time forward for free.

Why?

Because they become my beta readers, and many of them read my books and review them without me even having to ask. As a side note, I *never* ask them to give me a good review or even suggest they do so. If they review, I want their reviews to be authentic. I always hope the reviews will be positive, but how many stars they give each book is up to them. I'd rather have honest reviews than dishonest ones, and besides, it's unethical to pressure someone into giving you a good review just because you gave them a free book.

The members of my main street team get all kinds of perks for participating in various things throughout the year.

<u>Some of the things they do are:</u>

- Vote on a new book cover
- Vote on which audiobook narrator they like the best
- Share my Facebook and social media posts
- Play games (more on this one in a minute)
- Participate in polls (such as how many books they read per week, what vendor they buy their books on, etc.)
- Give feedback on the first chapter or two of a new book I'm writing
- Beta read books before they are released
- Give me feedback on a new character after they've read the first book in the new series

The feedback they provide is fantastic, and because they're familiar with my books and how I write, it means even more. I can't tell you how many times I've had them vote on their favorite book narrator and they have unanimously chosen someone other than the person I thought would be best. It's valuable, priceless insight.

I'm a bit like Oprah when it comes to my readers, *if* Oprah was working with a much smaller budget. I can't give away cars, but I can give away plenty of other things. My street team gets really pumped about it, and I love doing it.

At the beginning of each year I post a points-based incentive for the year. Almost everything they do for me during the year has a certain amount of points attached to it. Voting on their favorite book cover might be worth 20 and playing a guessing game might be worth 10. We try to keep it fun and achievable for everyone.

<u>This is what I posted at the beginning of this year:</u>

Hello Team!

Let's talk about this year's Street Team All Star Points Extravaganza where we award various point amounts as you participate in games, activities, tasks, take part in polls/voting, etc. At the beginning of each month we'll total the points you've earned and award prizes to all those who have reached a point milestone for that month.

In addition, at the end of the year the street team member with the most points will receive a very special reward. I'll fly to your town or city, we'll have lunch at your favorite restaurant, and maybe you can even show me around the area while I'm there. The team member with the second highest number of points will get to chat with me by phone or on a video call.

To remain on the street team, each member must earn a minimum of 100 points by the end of each year, a number that should be easy for any active member of the team to achieve.

Below is the list of awards we're offering this year:

100 Points: 3 audiobook codes or one signed book of your choice
250 Points: Coffee mug or notebook
400 Points: Tote bag, $20 gift card, or bookends

600 Points: Bookish pair of earrings, necklace, or bracelet
750 Points: Book lover T-shirt
1,000 Points: Goodie box of items I've chosen from Australia

Each month, my assistant posts a couple of games to keep the team engaged, because some months I have a lot going on, and others I don't, so having a game at the beginning and the middle of each month helps to keep them involved.

At the beginning of the month, we post a trivia game, and in the middle of the month, we have them guess how many jellybeans (and other items) are in a jar. They get points for playing and for getting the answer(s) right. I also play a game where I'll post ten facts about myself from time to time. Eight of the facts are true, and two are lies, and they have to guess which two are lies.

Here is an example of one of my recent trivia games:

Good Morning, Team! It's time for another round of "match the author facts" trivia game. I'll post nine questions below, and it's up to you to guess which question relates to which author.

AUTHOR ANSWERS:

Nora Roberts

James Patterson

Stephen King

Lee Child

John Grisham

Patricia Cornwell

Sue Grafton

David Baldacci

Mary Higgins Clark

Dean Koontz

QUESTIONS:

1. Which author's favorite childhood book was Peter Pan?
2. Which author wrote his/her first novel at the age of 18?
3. Which two authors were lawyers before they became authors?
4. Which author wrote romance and thriller novels under a pseudonym when he/she was just starting out?
5. Who worked as a director for a TV show for almost 20 years before becoming an author?
6. Which author's parents owned a pub when he/she was growing up?
7. Which author attended Catholic school?
8. Which author suffers from bipolar disorder?
9. Which author was accused of vandalism when he/she started signing his/her own books in an Australian bookstore?

(10 points for playing, +3 per correct answer)

By the way, if you're wondering what the answers are to the questions above:

1. James Patterson
2. Sue Grafton
3. David Baldacci and John Grisham
4. Dean Koontz
5. Lee Child
6. Mary Higgins Clark
7. Nora Roberts
8. Patricia Cornwell
9. Stephen King

In addition to games, I like to connect to the team members on more of a personal level, and this can be done without getting too personal. I'll share photos of what I've been up to (maybe scenic photos from a trip) and allow them to do the same. They also love sharing pet and children/grandchildren photos.

At Christmastime, I have them take photos of their decor using one of my most recent books in the photo, and then the rest of the team gets to vote on their favorite.

At the end of each year, I vet the main group and remove anyone who hasn't participated that year. And then on the newbie team, I advance the members who have been the most active that year to the main team.

CHAPTER 29

HEAR, HEAR: THE POWER OF NEWSLETTERS

If I could go back in time, one of the things I would tell my newbie writer self would be to focus more on building my newsletter, but not just on building it up from nothing—building it up with readers who consistently click and purchase my books, because those are the subscribers who matter the most. They're your gold-star subscribers, the ones who have signed up for your newsletter because they love your books and are invested in you as an author.

<u>If you don't already have a newsletter host, here are the two I recommend:</u>

Mailerlite is FREE for up to 1,000 subscribers and then it goes up from there. For 10,000 subscribers, it's only $50 a month at the moment. Their templates are easy to use and understand, and this is what I use to send newsletters to my primary email list.

Mailchimp is FREE for up to 2,000 subscribers. This includes one audience and a domain. They also have various other packages to choose from that offer more.

"A fan who signs up for your newsletter is trusting you to create a relationship with them that's not just based on them buying your books."

<u>Newsletter Q&A</u>

1. What are the two main styles of newsletters?

I find newsletters fall into two main categories most of the time: single focus and multi focus.

A single-focus newsletter is usually isolated to one main theme. Examples of this would be announcing your newest book is available for purchase, telling readers about a multi-author promo you're involved in, or sending an email out to promote a special deal such as a Black Friday sale.

A multi-focus email is usually divided into sections with different themes for each section. One section will usually contain information about your books, and other sections can be created to engage with your audience. This is so important because a fan who signs up for your newsletter is trusting you to create a relationship with them that's not just based on them buying your books.

They're investing in *you*, and you need to invest in them (more on this in a minute).

2.   How often should I send a newsletter?

Most authors I know send newsletters out once or twice a month. If you are able to send them on the same day(s) each month, I suggest doing it so you create a schedule for yourself.

I send my main newsletter out once each month. It is always a multi-focus email. I then send a second email if I'm involved in a giveaway, running an incentive, or if I am in an exclusive promotion.

I've heard some authors say they only send newsletters out when they have a new book, and I don't recommend doing it this way.

If you put a book out every three to six months, there's a big gap of time where you risk falling out of your readers radar.

I also don't think emails should ever be sent just to say, "BUY MY BOOK!"

Writers who do this are missing the chance to connect with their readers in a way that will keep them on your list and engaged instead of hitting the *Unsubscribe* button.

3.   What content ideas should I consider for my newsletter?

- Pre-order information/links
- Book cover reveal
- New release alert
- Giveaways
- Polls
- Sample chapters
- Book humor/memes/bookish jokes
- Requests for ARC reviewers or street team members
- Games
- Recipes

4. What are a few ideas for interactive games I can play with my readers?

What Happens Next?—In anticipation for a pre-order or upcoming new release, I'll send the first chapter or two of the upcoming book to get subscribers invested in it.

I always put the murder in the first chapter of my books, so I'll post that chapter for them to read and say: "Who do you think murdered [name of character] and why?"

I offer a $20 gift card or another equivalent gift to the subscriber with the most creative answer. All they need to do to enter is reply to the email. You wouldn't believe some of the hilarious responses. Some of my readers spend a lot of time coming up with interesting ideas, and I have so much fun reading their entries.

Scavenger Hunt—In the first month of a new book release, I'll put a scavenger hunt in my newsletter. Subscribers search the book for the answers and fill out a Google Form, and then we have a $20 drawing for all those who got the answers right.

As a side note here, somewhere on the newsletter or Google Form you need to say: No purchase necessary to enter (for legal reasons). I rarely have anyone email me about this, but when they do, it's always nice to be able to say it was included on the form, and all they need to do is fill out the form with their name to be entered in the contest.

Mystery/Thriller Author Trivia—This is the same game I play with my street team (see the section above for sample questions), and I offer a gift card and ask them to reply to the newsletter with their answers.

Who Designed It Best?—This is a fun game where you ask your readers to take a photo of your newest book in any creative setting.

It can be the print version or a photo of the cover from the first page of the book on their eReader. The submission that you like the best, or even the top three you like the best, receive a prize (maybe even something related to the book).

For an easy way to choose contest winners, use Random.org.

5.   What are some ideas of things to give away aside from books?

If you like buying in bulk, I'd suggest Discount Mugs as a great place to find cool items you can put your logo on. They have a lot more than just mugs, and they are one of the cheapest places to buy items in bulk, especially when you choose items from their clearance section.

If you buy single items, I suggest Amazon, especially if you have Amazon Prime. I also like Zazzle because I can create items using my own logos, and if you pay for Zazzle Black, which is currently $30 a year, you get free shipping. They almost always have a coupon code you can use that's at least 20% off.

As far as what to give away, I recently polled my Facebook followers, and these are the items they asked for the most:

- Mugs
- Magnetic bookmarks
- Secret compartment books
- Book lights
- Slippers (a bit strange, but okaaaay)
- Jewelry
- Scarves
- Plant pots
- Hats

- Kitchen towels
- Gift cards
- T-shirts
- Key chains
- Bookends
- Aprons
- Tote bags/shopping bags
- Signed books
- Oven mitts
- Jigsaw puzzles
- Book stationary
- Magnets
- Socks
- Serving platters
- Coasters
- Water bottles
- Book stands
- Notepads
- Ornaments
- Blankets

6. What polls or questions can I ask my subscribers to get them engaged in my newsletter?

- How do you read books? (paperback, hardback, eBook)
- What platform do you read on? (Amazon, Barnes & Noble, Kobo, Apple Books, etc.)
- What was the last book you read?
- What's the scariest book you've ever read?
- Who is your favorite author?
- Which book made you cry?

- If you could live in any book setting, which one would it be and why?
- If you could be a character from any book, who would it be?
- What author would you love to have lunch with?
- What is the first book you remember reading?
- Have you read a book more than once? If so, which one?
- What is the saddest book you've ever read?
- Which book made you laugh out loud?
- Do you read one book at a time or several at once?
- What genre(s) do you read besides mysteries and thrillers?
- What is the best book cover you've ever seen?
- What is your favorite snack to eat or drink to have while reading?
- Have you ever met a famous author? If so, who?
- Has a book ever changed your life? If so, how?
- What book would you like to become a TV series or movie?
- What movie/TV show was almost as good as the book?
- What movie/TV show was nothing like the book?
- What attracts you to a book?
- How many books do you read each month on average?
- Do you think books are better, the same, or worse than they used to be?
- Are there any books you haven't been able to finish? Why?
- Do you display books on a bookshelf or have a virtual library?
- Do you go to the library?
- What book twist shocked you?

7. How do I engage with my subscribers without getting too personal about my life?

At the beginning of the newsletter I send out each month, I write a paragraph about what's been going on in my life, and I talk to my readers about their lives as well. I always include a photo of some kind, which you can easily do without making it too personal.

Since I live in Australia at least half of the year, there are a lot of photos I can send that my readers enjoy seeing—crocodiles, kangaroos, wallabies, koalas, quokkas, sunsets, ocean, birds, rainforest, historical locations … you get the idea.

Think of the place you live. Odds are a great deal of your subscribers will never go there in their lifetime. What is unique about your town/city that you can show them? Do you have pets? Readers LOVE connecting with you about their pets (that just gave me an idea about doing a *Pet of the Month* feature).

I talk to my readers about where I am and what I'm doing, but you don't have to get super personal to establish a connection with your readers. Even sharing a little information makes them feel like they are a part of your journey.

It's fine to talk about yourself briefly in your newsletters, but remember, it isn't and shouldn't be all about you. It should also be about them. Think of your readers as part of your team. Instead of using the word "I," consider using the word "you" more often instead.

8. How do I find new subscribers?

The best way to get free, organic subscribers is to make sure to include a link to your newsletter at the back of every book you publish. To give readers an incentive to sign up, you can include a reader magnet, like giving them a free book for signing up to your newsletter list. Another free idea is to include a pop-up newsletter subscription box on the main page of your author website if you have one.

Some writers offer an exclusive reader magnet that you can't get anywhere else. One example of this is to give new subscribers a prequel of one of your books. I offer two books, the first in two of my popular series.

A great way to add new subscribers is to run book-related giveaways. You can do this on any of your social media accounts. I create the giveaway on Google Forms. I give away cool things like bookish socks or a book mug, and I drop-ship from sites like Amazon and Zazzle, so the shipping is free. I cap the reward to $20 or less because you don't need to give away the whole kit-and-kaboodle to get people to sign up.

When offering giveaways for sign-ups, I still get people on my list here and there who never open and never click. We keep a close eye on them and weed out anyone who isn't active after several months.

<u>When you are running a giveaway to try and gain new followers, there are a couple of important things to note:</u>

The first is … thou shalt not give away non-bookish prizes! You only want subscribers who are actual readers, and more specifically, those who read mystery and thriller books. Sure, you'll still get some subscribers here and there who just want to win something, and they don't care what it is. One way I keep them out of my mailing list is to ask a question on Google Forms that's book-related like:

What book are you currently reading?

If they say "nothing" or leave it blank, I usually don't add them to my newsletter.

You also can't just add everyone to your newsletter list without their permission. How you get around this is by creating a question on the Google Form. Mine is:

Would you like to be part of Cheryl Bradshaw's mailing list? (We only send newsletters once or twice a month, and your email and personal information is always kept private!)

- Yes
- No
- I already subscribe

If they say no, you CANNOT add them to your newsletter list.

Another way to get subscribers is to get involved in some of the paid promotion sites that run contests and collect the name and email of anyone who enters. At the end of the promotion these lists are shared with you and all of the other authors involved in the giveaway. I do these from time to time, and they've been successful, but I also feel it's best to keep working on gaining new followers on your own whenever you can.

One site that offers multi-offer promotions is BookSweeps.

Prolific Works is another site where you can sign up for multi-author promotions.

And if you prefer not to use Google Forms, Rafflecopter is another great place to create author giveaways.

9. How do I keep new subscribers when I find them?

Make sure you connect with new subscribers as soon as possible after they've signed up for your newsletter. It's important to send something out right away so you can engage the subscriber and so you start to build an author/subscriber relationship.

My new readers receive five emails from me after they sign up (one each week) BEFORE I add them to my regular email newsletters that go out a couple of times each month. My goal with these emails is to build a relationship first before I ask them to make a purchase.

Here's how mine work.

EMAIL 1: Introduction

New subscribers come to me in a variety of ways, and I never assume they have read my books or that they are familiar with who I am, even though most of them are familiar with me and my work. If I want them to become interested in my books, it's up to me to take their hand and help them on their way.

In email one, I talk about my writing background, and I make it personal. This was really hard for me to do at first because I am a very private person. But I recently took a course on newsletters and customer engagement, and the course convinced me to restructure the current method I'd been using. As a side note, I'd suggest always asking a question at the end of your main messages to further the new connection you're trying to make with your reader.

Email 1 looks like this:

When I was around eight years of age, I started making up stories to tell my younger sister when we went to bed each night. Her favorite was Loin Ta, a fairy tale about two kids who were given a couple special pieces of gum while out trick-or-treating. When they popped the gum into their mouths they were transported to a magical place where they grew up to be king and queen, ruling over all the land.

I remember my mother being called into the principal's office when I was in elementary school and my teacher expressing concern over the Judy Blume books I was reading, which she believed were far too advanced for my age. Maybe they were, but my mother always encouraged my love of reading. By the time I was in high school, I'd leave my honor's English class and head over to my Algebra I class, which I had to take THREE times, my freshman, sophomore, and junior year ... true story! It's safe to say, math has never been my friend. My father once said, "If you get a C in math, I consider it an A. If you get a C in English, I consider it an F." And since I was given cold, hard cash for good grades, those words made all the difference!

When I checked out my first Agatha Christie novel at the library as a teen, I was smitten. No one wrote like she did, and in that moment, I knew crime fiction was the genre I wanted to write in for the rest of my life. I should have started writing novels then, but often times life's path involves a few bumps and bruises before we stumble upon our true calling. I was a Montessori teacher, computer teacher, vice president of a secret shopping company, and a real estate agent before I found my way back to what I'm most passionate about in life—writing.

What's the best mystery or thriller novel you've ever read? Or what novel changed your life in some profound way? Hit reply and let me know. I monitor this inbox myself, and even though I'm not always able to reply, I read every message. It means a lot to me that you're here!

Talk to you soon,
Cheryl Bradshaw

EMAIL 2: Where Am I Now?

In my second email, I talk about where I live and how I came to be here. And just like the first email, this one should be personal as well. I'd suggest you not copy/paste your author biography here, and instead, write something fresh and new, something just for this newsletter audience. Again, try to make it as personal as you're comfortable with if you can. Mine turned out a lot more personal than I was comfortable with at first, but sometimes that's a good thing because I truly believe you create a better connection with others when you share your truth. It also pushed me out of my comfort zone, something this awkward introvert is always working on!

<u>Email 2 looks like this:</u>

I had a health scare a few years ago when I learned I am considered high risk for getting breast cancer. The day my doctor gave me the news, it changed my perspective on life. I started thinking about all of the things I've always wanted to do that I haven't done yet, and I questioned myself about why I hadn't don't those things.

As I considered what I wanted most out of the rest of my life, I decided to do something way out of my introverted comfort zone. Traveling to another country all by myself was at the top of my bucket list. I did my research and decided to head to Australia, which came as a shock to many of my family and friends. Many believed I would never do it in the end … they were wrong.

I arrived in tropical Cairns, Australia, a place where the great barrier reef meets the rainforest, having no idea the six-week trip would change the course of my life forever. On day five I was sitting in a café working on my newest book, and an Australian guy came over to my table and said, "Hi." That was almost three years ago, and now I split my time between Australia and the US.

Speaking of the US, there are so many states I haven't been to yet, and I'd like to visit them all over the next several years. What's something unique or interesting about the town or city where you live? Hit reply and let me know.

In my next email, I'll send you a link to download one of my mystery books for free.

Have a great day,
Cheryl Bradshaw

EMAIL 3: Introduction to My First Mystery Series

In the third email, I start talking about what I write, and I give readers an overview of one of my main characters. This is how that email is set up.

Step One: I introduce my main character, Sloane Monroe, and I talk about my vision when I created her, who she is, what makes her tick, and a little about the series itself. When writing your own email, I'd suggest keeping it to one or two paragraphs rather than making it too lengthy.

Step Two: I post the cover of the first book in the Sloane Monroe series, provide the description, and include a link for them to download the book for free.

EMAIL 4: Introduction to My Supernatural Suspense Mystery Series

This email is set up exactly like Email 3 except I talk about the supernatural series instead. I offer them the first book in that series free as well.

EMAIL 5: Introduction to My New Mystery Series

This email is also set up in a similar way to emails 3-4, except, instead of linking them to a free book, I include the first chapter of the first book in my new Georgiana Germaine series and then I include links to purchase that book. Note—this is the first time in over a month of them receiving emails from me that I give them the opportunity to buy something. Why? One main principle. With subscribers, you always build trust *first* and sell second.

Once they have received email 5, they are added to my main newsletter subscriber list where they start receiving the same emails my existing subscribers receive.

And for an entire book dedicated to newsletter marketing, check out Tammi Labrecque's book called *Newsletter Ninja*. It's packed with tips on how to start a newsletter and how to take it to the next level.

CHAPTER 30

ALL SYSTEMS GO: PUBLISHING CHECKLIST

Your book is finished, you've paid for a professional editor, a proofer, formatter, and you have a classy book cover. Now it's time to shift gears and focus on your book's release. Let's talk about some basic things you should consider doing as part of your publishing checklist.

One to Three Months Before Publishing

1. Replace your Facebook banner with a new one promoting the new/upcoming book and any available links if it's on pre-order.
2. Post a cover reveal of your book on all social media and in your newsletter.
3. Email your mailing list and get your subscribers excited about the upcoming book by offering them things like reading the first one or two chapters before the book comes out and by introducing them to the storyline and characters in the book.

4. Contact book bloggers to set up tour dates. On Booksirens Mystery Reviewers site you can search through a range of book bloggers who are currently accepting reviews.

5. Schedule blog tours. Organizing a blog tour on your own can be really labor intensive. There are a lot of blog tour companies that will promote your book on several different blogs for a modest price. For a great list of blog tour promoters and what packages they offer, check out Ramona Morrow Books.

6. Once your title is up for pre-order or goes on sale, claim your book at Amazon Author Central.

Two to Four Weeks Before Publishing

1. Update your website with information about the new book and any other relevant book product pages.

    If this isn't the first book you've published, you'll want to take advantage of spreading the information about your newest release wherever you can. One simple way you can do this is by making sure it's mentioned on the pages of your other books.

    On Amazon, a lot of authors don't take advantage of writing things in any areas other than the book's description section. In the "from the author section" you can do things like connect with your readers by telling them the inspiration behind the story you just wrote, or you can use this section to list out your books or book series in order by saying something like:

    Book Series in Order by [Your Name] and then list the books out in numerical order.

    I try to put the order of my books in as many places as possible and on as many sites as possible. I find readers are often confused about what book comes next, even when the books are linked in order at the top of the product page and easy to see. Even so, it's our job to make their life easier in any way we can.

2. Create promotional graphics on a site like BookBrush and two weeks before the book's release, start sharing a different graphic quote from your book on your social media sites every day. Here are two examples from one of my recent book releases.

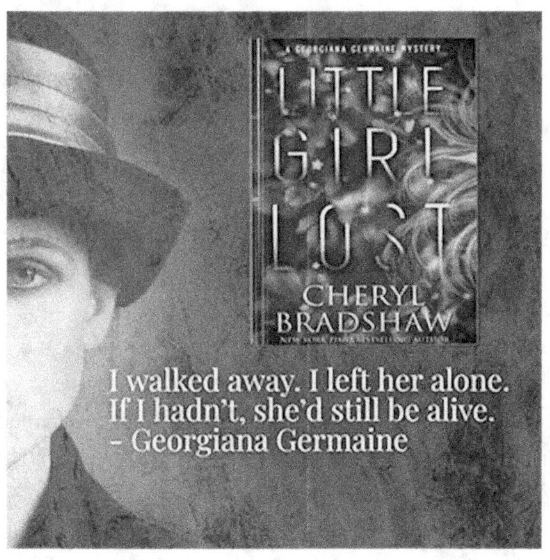

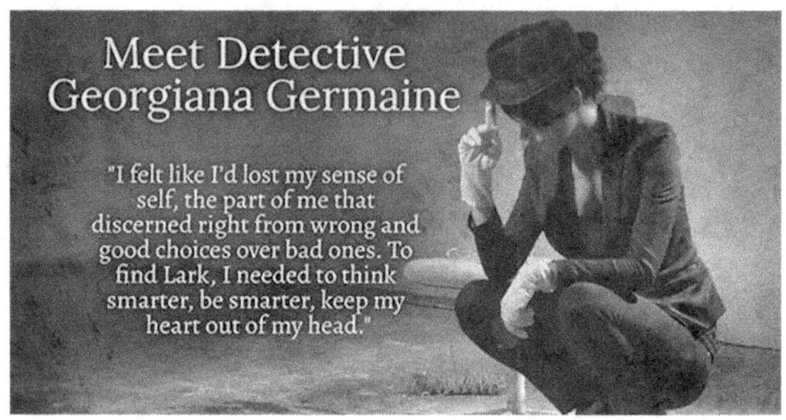

3. Send ARC's to your beta reader and/or street team members.

4. Create a giveaway to send to your newsletter followers and to post on your social media offering something to those who pre-order the book.

As a side note here, when you run a giveaway, you must allow everyone to enter the giveaway whether they've purchased the book or not. To make sure you're obeying the law, you need to put a disclaimer at the bottom of your offer that says something like *No Purchase Necessary to Enter.*

I create a giveaway using Google Forms. If you're short on cash or looking for a free way to have a giveaway, ask another author that writes in the same genre if they will offer one of their full-price books to your readers as a gift to any of your readers who pre-order your book. They'll usually say yes because it's a great way for them to cross-promote themselves to your readers without spending money to do it. The author doesn't have to discount their book anywhere either. All they need to do is to create a download link on a site like BookFunnel.

5. Set an advertising budget and then create targeted ads on Facebook, Amazon Advertising, BookBub, etc. Run test ad graphics on Facebook where you test a handful of different graphics to see which one gets the most clicks. I like to test without the book cover on the graphic first so I get a good idea of which graphic is more appealing to my target audience.

Publishing Day

1. Post about your book's release on all social media outlets.
2. Create another giveaway in your newsletter and on social media sites. I like to create a scavenger hunt where readers who have purchased the book can find answers to questions by searching the book, and I'll give away something fun to go along with that to a few winners.

An example of a question I might ask: At the beginning of Chapter 41, who does Georgiana hit with her Jeep?

1. Change your Facebook banner. Refreshing the banner on release day helps readers realize something has changed. Before, the book was on pre-order. Now, the new banner lets them know release day is finally here.
2. Email your beta readers/street team and let them know it's time to post their reviews.
3. If you're in Kindle Unlimited, plan out a strategy to make the most of your five free days. I tend to split them up over two different weekends. Three on a Friday-Sunday, and the remaining two on a Saturday-Sunday.

First Three Months of Release

I like to do a soft release of my book first, meaning I don't discount the book's price right away, prior to, or during the initial release. The reason I don't is because I work hard to promote the book before it's out to my core fan base, and I don't want to drop the price two weeks after they've purchased it at $5.99 to $0.99.

This works well for me, but if I was an author just starting out, my strategy would be a lot different. I would try publishing the book at $0.99 at first and stacking small ads for 2-4 weeks after the book's release date. At that point, I would think about hiking up the price of the book.

Three to Six Months After Release

A few months after the book's release, I start my hard release plans to give the book a strong push. I'll apply for a BookBub feature at $0.99 (I don't reduce the price to free for the first year unless I'm in KDP Select). If a BookBub feature is confirmed, I stack smaller ads around it, starting a week before the BookBub ad and ending two to three weeks later just to stretch the low ranking out as long as I can.

I usually run smaller ads every other day on places like Robin Reads, Freebooksy, and Kindle Nation Daily. Along with this, I run targeted ads, and I'll spend more than I usually do on push week.

What if you don't get a BookBub?

If you apply for a BookBub ad and don't get accepted, purchase some of the other less spendier options and stack promos around it.

CHAPTER 31

BIG PIMPING:
FACEBOOK ADS

I've tried all different kinds of ads, and I've found Facebook Ads to be the most effective. I've taken a few courses and spent a lot of time learning about what works and what doesn't. Over the years I've tested many different targets, including authors, book pages, bookstores, book publishers, TV shows, movies, etc. to test which offer the most successful ROI (return on investment).

The frustrating thing about Facebook Ads is that Facebook is always making upgrades and changes to their platform, and sometimes you have to start from scratch and relearn something you had just about perfected. For that reason, I'm not going to include a step-by-step process on how to create ads, but I will offer a few tips and suggest some fantastic books to read that cover how to create and maintain ads.

On Facebook, you can run ads a couple of different ways. The first is to boost a post on your author page. The second is by going through Ads Manager. I do both, but the bulk of my ads are created through Ads Manager because I am always trying to find new readers. I boost ads through my author page when I have a new book releasing and want to target my existing followers.

Before you start creating ads, I suggest putting a list together of targets so you can run tests and see which targets perform better than others. What you want is to end up with a good list of targets who not only have a decent CPC (cost per click), but also generate sales.

<u>These targets should include:</u>

- Authors who write similar to you
- Popular TV shows and movies in your genre
- Genre-specific targets like mystery fiction and detective fiction
- Popular book sites like BookBub and GoodreadsPopular book publishing sites like Barnes & Noble, Apple Books, and Kobo

The first thing I do when I am creating an ad through Ads Manager for a new book is to test at least six different graphics to see which one gets the most clicks. I do this prior to adding the book to the image.

While we're on the subject of graphics, let's talk about where to get them. These sites are among the most popular:

- depositphotos
- shutterstock
- iStock
- Megapixl
- dreamstime

Now let's take a look at six images I downloaded on depositphotos.

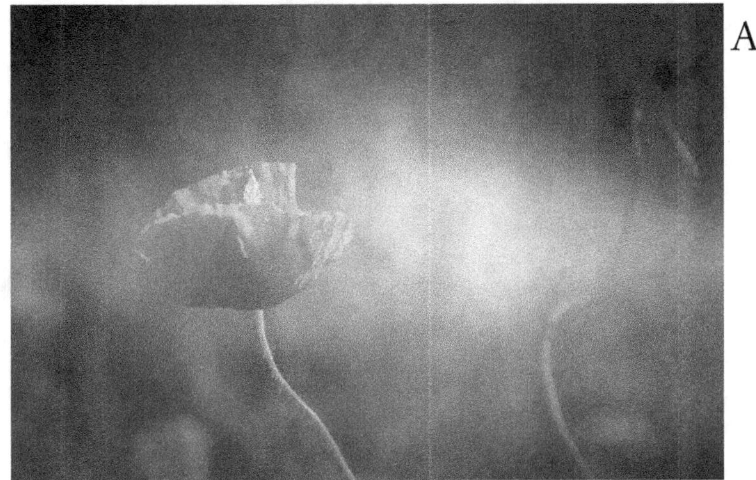
A

B

C

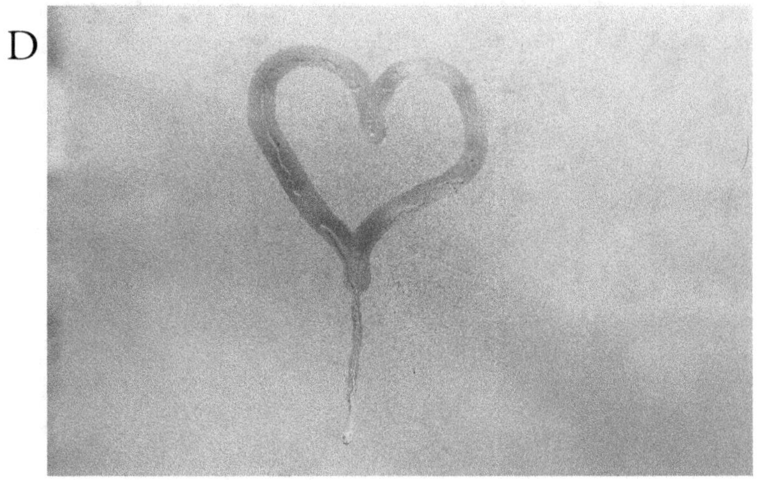

D

E

F

"Clicks don't always generate sales. That's why testing is so important."

The six images above were in my first test group for a book I recently released. I like to use a variation of themes, and that's why I went with a little girl, a flower, and hearts. In the first chapter of the book a child is kidnapped after her father is murdered so the children in these graphics fit in nicely with the tone and theme of the book.

Looking at the images, which one do you think had the lowest CPC (cost per click) after one month?

For this test, I ran two separate ads. Both were shown to women age 47+ in the United States. One of the targets I used was a male mystery author. The other target was three female mystery authors. With that in mind, does it change the graphic you think performed the best? Let's find out if you're right.

In both ads, E had the lowest CPC's of .16 and .20. In second place was B at .21 and .26, and in third place was F at .24 and .25.

How did you do? Were you right?

I initially thought F would be the best because of its vibrant colors and the fact it almost looks like a painting, something my female readers tend to like. This is why I test so much. My favorite won't always be a reader's favorite, and their opinion is the only one that matters here.

I removed A, C, D after my initial test, and then added the book cover to ads B, E, F. To date, E is still doing the best, but all three graphics are running close in cost to each other at .16, .20, .21. If you're wondering why I don't pause .20 and .21, and just use the cheapest, I'll tell you. Clicks don't always generate sales. I could get more clicks on a .16 ad, but more sales on the .21 ad. That's why testing is so important.

Another thing I want to point out is that you should create ads for your top three performers and try many different targets individually because some targets will like a different graphic than the other target. For example, let's say I target James Patterson, and his audience likes the F graphic the best. Then I target Sue Grafton, and her audience liked F, but B had a lower CPC.

This is one of the ads I am running today:

My sister would call this ad a "Basic Bitch." It's simple. I know. There's no text, just the graphic and the book. Why do I keep it simple? Facebook favors clean simplicity with their ads. What they don't like is a lot of text in the ad. If they think there's too much going on, your ad might still get served, and you'll still spend the daily amount you set, but the ad won't get as many impressions. For this reason, I don't put any text in most of my ads. I put it in the product description.

The book in the ad on the previous page is currently selling at full price of $5.99 because it's new, but I also run a lot of ads offering readers discounts for some of my other books because my objective is to keep reaching new readers who have never heard of me or read my books. New readers often hesitate before paying $5.99 for an author they've never heard of before, but not always. If you have great reviews and social proof on your landing page, readers still consider buying the book.

Some of my most successful ads targeted to new readers are my 50% off ads for the first books in my other two series, and this one on the next page is for my supernatural suspense that's in KU for a few months at the moment.

The graphic for *Grayson Manor Haunting* is one I've used a lot in the last two years because it is almost always in the top two performers across all targets.

Murderous Mysteries
Sponsored · 🌐

•••

When Addison Lockhart inherits Grayson Manor
after her mother's untimely death, she unlocks a
dark family secret that's been kept hidden for
over fifty years

Grayson Manor Haunting, Book 1, Addison
Lockhart Series

> Amazon: https://amzn.to/2Z2cFFz
> Audible: https://amzn.to/2XpwLta
> Paperback: https://amzn.to/2KiSbEg

   59   5 Comments 13 Shares

 Like    Comment   Share

Here are some helpful suggestions for setting up an ad like this:

- If you can create the ad on a page other than your author page, I highly recommend doing so. As you can see from the graphic, the ad is sponsored by Murderous Mysteries, a new group I created last year. If you create your own page, make sure you're always adding content to the page that is not related to you or your books. I post a variety of different things on there.

- Keep the text in the primary text section of the ad short and sweet. Create an enticing blurb that's between 2-4 lines. Make sure to include the book's name. You might be thinking, "Why? The name of the book is in the graphic." You're right. It is. But after years of doing these ads, any time I don't include the name of the book, I get people asking me for the name of the book in the comments. Go figure.

- Include any/all links in a clean, clear, precise way. Try to make the landing page clickable in as few clicks as possible. I'd suggest no more than two clicks to get to the page where they can buy your book. When a reader clicks, the ad should either take them straight to the vendor site like Amazon where they can download the book, or to your website where they can purchase/download from there, or to a place like Books2Read where they can choose their store and buy the book with one more click.

- I usually choose the "Learn More" button for the ad, and I've linked this one to Amazon because the series is exclusive in KU at the moment.

- In the Headline field, I've included the deal I'm offering: **50% Off. Limited Time**. It's short and sweet, and there's no confusion about the offer.

<u>Tips and Tricks when setting up your ad in Ads Manager:</u>

I'm going to take you through the basics of what works best for me on my ads, and I would encourage you to test different options to see what works best for you.

1. <u>Ad Creation</u>: The first thing you'll do when you go into Ads Manager to set up a new ad is to choose the **Create** button, which should be a green tab on the upper left-hand side of your screen.

2. <u>Create New Campaign</u>: Here I choose **Auction** and then **Traffic**. You can also name your campaign in this section. Make sure to give the campaign a name that helps you remember what's in the ad you created. For example, on the ad above, I named it: **GMH—Ghost Mysteries—500K—10-20**. GMH is the initials for the name of the book: Grayson Manor Haunting. Ghost Mysteries is the target, 500K is the audience size, and 10-20 is the date the ad was created.

3. <u>Setting a Campaign Budget/Daily Budget</u>: In the next section you can set your campaign or daily budget. If the ad is new and you're running tests, you may want to start out at $5 per day and then scale up from there after you narrow down which ads are the most successful.

4. <u>Traffic/Audience/Targeting</u>: You always want to drive traffic to a website, which is where you'll send those who click on your ad. This will be your book product page or a page clickable to the product page.

I usually skip the next two sections for **Dynamic Creative** and **Offer**, and if you've already set your **Budget & Schedule** on the previous page, you can skip this too.

In the **Audience** section you will first choose the location where your ad will be targeted. I would suggest choosing one location per ad, meaning United States only instead of United States, Canada, and Australia. Why? Several reasons, but ads tend to perform better when targeting them one location at a time, and I have found that the graphic that does best in the US is not always the same as the graphic that does the best in Canada, etc.

Have you ever noticed authors like Stephen King will have one book cover for some countries and a different book cover for others? Now you know why.

Setting the age and gender for your ad is up to you and will depend on your core demographic. If you don't know what your core demographic is, this is a great way to test out different ages/genders, which you can narrow down later when you look at results. More on this in a minute.

Now we get to the fun part: **Detailed Targeting**. This is where you can test all the different targets I discussed at the beginning of this chapter. Testing more popular authors will result in a higher CPC, but that doesn't mean you shouldn't try them out.

Let's say you decide to test a television show like *CSI: Miami*. You'll want to narrow this down further because only a portion of those who watch the show also read books, and you want an audience that clicks on the ads for the right reasons, and who aren't curious lookey-loo's (all click and no purchase).

How do you narrow an audience? Select the **Narrow Audience** tab, and it will say "and must also match," and this is where you enter one or more book-related options like: BookBub, Goodreads, eBooks, Mystery Fiction, Amazon Kindle, or Barnes & Noble Nook.

Now the ad will be shown to all those who like *CSI: Miami* AND the second option you chose.

Next you'll choose your placements, and Facebook loves to try and get you to select automatic placements, but I almost always choose Manual Placements. The reason is because most of my core demographic is older and on Facebook. Many of them are not on Instagram. I've noticed when I include Instagram, I get a lot of likes on the ad itself but not as many purchases. I also don't like the ads to be displayed in Messenger, and I have not found Audience Network works in my favor.

Finally, we come to **Optimization & Delivery**, and for this I stick with Link Clicks.

5. On the last page (you're almost there!!!) you'll first select your **Identity**. If you only have a Facebook author page, that's what you'll select. If you have another bookish fan page, you can also choose to select that page instead.

On **Ad Setup**, you'll choose either a single image or video, carousel, or collection. I have been trying to improve the performance of my carousel ads, but single image ads/videos work best for me.

Once you select **Add Image**, it will pull up any/all images you've used in the past, or you can upload a new one. Select your image and then click the Next button.

I'd also suggest clicking the Edit button below the image, then Edit Media, going into the square design and any others you would like to check and making any adjustments needed there so your ad displays what you want it to properly. Make sure you click the Save button once you're finished.

Enter in the rest of your ad information, and when you're finished, hit the Publish button.

Voila! Your ad has now been created.

Before I end this section, I want to talk about the valuable information Facebook offers when you create these ads. When you're in Ads Manager on your campaigns page, click on the campaign you would like more information about. On the right side of the page you'll see a slim, vertical gray bar with four icons. Right below the X is an icon called "See Charts." Click on this and you will be able to get more specific information about your ad, including the ad's performance, demographics, placement, and delivery. I use the demographics option to get a good idea of whether the ad is targeting the right age group, etc.

Looking at the demographics of one of my ads below, you can see I get the most clicks at 55+ and do the very best at 65+. This let me know I needed to adjust the ad, which I changed to 55+.

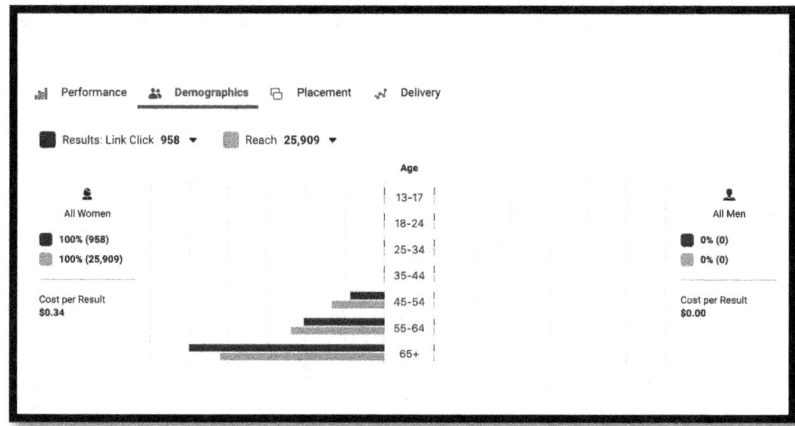

I hope everything in this chapter wasn't too overwhelming and that it was easy enough to understand. I could write an entire book on this topic alone. For more detailed information on ad creation, I highly recommend the book *Help! My Facebook Ads Suck,* by Mal and Jill Cooper.

CHAPTER 32

IT'S TRICKY: AMAZON ADS

As I'm sitting here writing this section, the RUN DMC song "It's Tricky" is playing in my head because that sums up how I feel about Amazon ads. I have been running ads through Amazon Advertising since 2016, and I still feel like I have a lot to learn. The tricky thing about these ads is that they don't utilize the entire budget you set per day like Facebook and BookBub ads do. Sometimes I can figure out why, which usually has to do with me needing to up my bids and tweaking my targets. Other times, I have no idea why some ads are given an all-access pass and others fall flat.

The bulk of the ads I run are through the US, but I like to add a few here and there each month in other countries as well. I've heard other authors say that it's not worth it to advertise in the other countries, but I am starting to get a bit of traction, especially with books in Kindle Unlimited, and on the plus side, ads in other countries are cheaper than those in the US … at the moment.

Speaking of cheap and not cheap, the mystery/thriller category is very competitive. Four years ago, I could bid on many authors for around .25 and still get clicks. Now some of those same authors might cost me $1 to $2 per click. Why? Because more authors are running Facebook ads now than they were back then, so there's a lot more competition when it comes to bidding.

I'm not going to walk you through how to create an ad on the Amazon Advertising platform if you're a beginner (I'll recommend some books to read that go into it in more detail at the end of this section), but I would like to give you some tips on targeting and bids.

Targeting

- Target the authors in your "customers who bought this item also also bought" list on your Amazon product pages from the section of your book page called "Customers Who Bought This Item Also Bought," and as a side note, I would not recommend targeting authors in the "Products Related to this Item" section because those are sponsored ads created by other authors and not necessarily similar books to yours.
- Target the authors on your Amazon Author Page, the page where your bio and books are listed. Those authors can be found on that page in the "Customers Also Bought Items By" section.
- Target the top 100 books and authors in your book categories. If your books are NOT in Kindle Unlimited, I would focus on the books in the top 100 that are not in KU because those readers are looking for free/discount/sale books that are in KU.

If you are in Kindle Unlimited, I suggest running two separate ads. Let's say you are creating an ad to target the top 100 books in the Mystery: Private Investigators category. Create one ad using all of the authors whose books appear in the top 100 list and are also in Kindle Unlimited, and create another ad targeting any books in the top 100 that are not in Kindle Unlimited. I suggest doing this because if you can generate several days of strong sales on the book you're advertising, Amazon might start recommending it to readers.

If you decide to target in other countries outside of the US, take note that the US top 100 in mystery will not be the same in other countries.

But you can view their top 100 lists just as easily as you can in the US:

Canada

Australia

United Kingdom

- Target yourself. Yes, you read that right. I still generate the most sales when I target myself, my book titles, and my series names. You should also take into consideration that some readers won't always spell your name right or your book's title, or your series name, so consider targeting similar versions. My Sloane Monroe series is often typed Sloan Monroe or Sloane Munroe, so I target both of those spellings too.
- Target the genres and subgenres you write in.
- Create a targeted list by creating a report of what keywords

resulted in a sale. I do this monthly. You can do it by going into the reports section (you can find this in the vertical, navy colored section to the left of the page), clicking **Create Report**, selecting the targeting option, filling in any other relevant information, and then clicking **Run Report**. Once it's created you can download it to Excel and look at which keywords perform the best.

There are several great books out there to help you learn how to create and run successful Amazon ads. Here are a few that I recommend:

Mastering Amazon Ads, Brian D. Meeks

Amazon Ads for Authors 2020, D M Potter

Amazon Ads Unleashed, Robert J. Ryan

And there's a great group on Facebook where writers can connect with each other about ad strategies: Authors Optimizing Amazon and Facebook Ads—Support Group

CHAPTER 33

SHE (AND HE) WORK HARD FOR THE MONEY: BOOKBUB ADS

BookBub is another advertising platform I am still working on mastering, but I have learned a lot since I first started advertising there, and I was part of their initial beta group before it officially launched.

The best advice I can give you about how to create successful BookBub ads would be to read *BookBub Ads Expert* by David Gaughran. He has invested a lot of time into figuring out what works and what doesn't, and he has more knowledge about their platform than anyone I've ever talked to about it.

BookBub's core audience likes sales, discounts, and freebies. If you want your ads to be successful, I recommend creating ads that are at least 50% off your regular purchase price. Free is king, .99 is queen, and 50% off and "new" are your prince and princess. You can expect to have the most success when you run ads for a free book.

Similar to Facebook Ads where you can reel someone in using engaging graphics and captivating text, BookBub Ads center around the graphic itself, and what's great is, unlike Facebook, you can write as much as you want on them.

Do's of BookBub Ads

- Keep the graphic clean and concise.
- Use no more than a few key elements for each ad, such as the book's cover, the deal price, and a "learn more" link. If you add words, like a tagline, keep it short.
- Target the right audience. Example: if your book is crime fiction, you should not be targeting cozy mystery readers.
- Keep the text on your ad short, sweet, and to the point.
- Use a background graphic that accentuates the book you're selling, and make sure it evokes the same tone and emotion as your book.
- Test. Test. Test. Expect to try several different graphic/test audiences before you find the perfect fit.

Don'ts of BookBub Ads

- Don't create a graphic that's too busy. You don't need to load your ad up with the book cover, the price, the book blurb, a "learn more" button, a review from a reader, a sentence about what the book is about, and an accolade about yourself such as "New York Times Best Selling Author."
- Choose only a few of these per ad. It's not about making a single graphic and cramming everything onto it. You can make several for the same book and use the one or two that tests the best.
- Don't target audiences or authors that aren't in line with the book you're selling.

- Don't include a book excerpt or a quote that's too long or too hard to read. Less = more.
- Avoid ads that leave the reader wondering what genre the book is. This often happens when ads are created without the book's cover, or that include the book's cover but are on the wrong background.
- Don't assume a creative font is the best way to go, especially when it's too slim or too hard to read.

I've Created My Test Ads. Now What?

Once your graphics have been created, you can test out various audiences to see which ones are the most successful. The first thing I do when I create new ad graphics is to test them all on a broader scale to see which graphic does better than the others. I do this by targeting specific genres first. Some of the genres we can test in mystery are:

- Psychological Thrillers
- Cozy Mysteries
- Crime Fiction
- Thrillers
- Historical Mysteries
- Romantic Suspense

I choose the genre that is the best fit for the book I want to promote and then I set a budget of $5 a day while I test the different graphics I've created. Similar to Facebook, I'll test a handful of different graphics for the same book and keep 1 or 2 of the best performers.

Now I need to find authors to test. I like to come up with a list of approximately 200 authors to search, which I'll find by looking through the "also boughts" section of the book I want to advertise and by looking at the current top 100 lists in that genre.

Of the 200, my goal is to narrow it down to 25-50 authors I feel are the best ones to test.

How do I know which authors are better to target than others?

The sweet spot is to target authors who have a following on BookBub (let's say 400 or more followers at minimum), but not a following that's too big (over 30k). Why? Authors with too few followers don't last long. You'll blow through them in a day or two. On the flip side, authors with too large of a following generally cost more money to target because you're not the only one targeting them—a lot of other authors are targeting them too.

With my list of 200 in front of me, I narrow down the list by going to BookBub's website. I start at the top of the list and enter the name of the author in the search bar.

Looking at a recent list I made for my ghost mystery series, the first name on the list was Stephen King. Before I typed in his name, I knew he'd have a massive following, but I was still curious about the exact size number. He has almost 850k followers to date, so I crossed him off and moved on to someone more suited to my needs and what I'm trying to achieve. I tried Deborah Harkness next. She had almost 15k followers, which is a much better size.

When I target her, I want to see a CTR (click through rate) of 2% or better. At 1%, I'll still try a few different graphics to see if I can get a better result. If not, I'll pause the ad. I'd also like to note that the better the deal, the higher CTR I want to see. If the book promotion is free or $0.99, I'm hoping for a 3% or higher CTR.

Targeting by Location

When you set up your ad, BookBub will automatically recommend regions and areas to target your book. I suggest trying various locations to see which ones are most successful for you, but I prefer to target one at a time. If I'm targeting Amazon US, for example, I won't target other countries, and if I'm targeting Barnes & Noble, I won't target Apple. I've found I'm more successful when I target everything separately. I've also found I often get a better CTR when I target other countries outside of the US. The thing you need to remember when doing that though is that those audiences aren't as large as the US market, so they won't last as long either.

Aside from featured ads and BookBub ads, I also use their Pre-Order Alerts and their Featured New Releases.

Pre-Order Alerts

I apply for pre-order alerts for almost every book I publish. If you have taken the time to build up your followers on BookBub, pre-order alerts can be an excellent way to make money right before the book's release.

At the moment, any author who has over 1,000 followers on BookBub is eligible to schedule a pre-order alert. The cost is a mere $0.02 per US follower. You can schedule your pre-order date between 7-30 days in the future. It just has to go out to your followers within a day of the book's release.

Featured New Releases

The best reason to run a Featured New Release Alert on BookBub is to give your book a huge push during launch week. If you schedule one and pad it with other ads you're running, you'll give your book its best chance at keeping a lower ranking longer than it would have otherwise.

You can schedule a Featured New Release up to six months before the book's release date. Once submitted, it will be reviewed, and you will be notified whether you've been selected. If selected, you'll choose a category to run the book in and then you'll pay for the feature. This promotion is a lot like a Featured Deal, except you have the ability of keeping the book at full price instead of discounting it.

CHAPTER 34

GO, FIGHT, WIN: WHERE TO ADVERTISE YOUR BOOK

I know how hard it can be to get visibility for your book when you're just starting out. Most authors don't have a big budget to spend in the beginning, and the hardest part is that if you don't "pay to play" nowadays, it's hard for your book to get noticed. And often times, even if you are spending a good chunk of money, it can *still* be hard to get your book noticed.

Think about your book like it's a good investment you've just made in the stock market. At first, you might only be able to buy one or two shares per month at $25 a share. That's fine. The goal is to keep going, sell more and more books over time, and then reinvest a portion of your earnings.

Because we all have different budgets to work with, I'm going to offer a variety of websites to try out, ranging from free to high-dollar sites like BookBub. At the moment, all of these sites are active, and I'll do my best to revise this list yearly.

FREE SITES TO PROMOTE ON

askDavid
For free books only.

Authors Den
You can create an account for free, but if you buy a gold membership, you get a higher amount of exposure.

Awesome Gang
It's free to promote your book here, or you can pay $10 to have your book featured on their front page for two days and have it sent out to their Facebook, Twitter, and email lists.

Bookangel
For free or $0.99 books.

Book Bongo
You can submit your book free on this site, but there's no guarantee they'll post it. They have paid options starting at $9.99.

Book Circle
Free or upgrade to a premium promo for $10. Book deals only.

Book Hippo
You need to register an account on their site to promote your book.

Book Praiser
You can create an account on their site and feature your books.

Content Mo
Free book promotion.

Digital Book Today

Free books must remain free for at least 24 hours. Fiction books must have an average rating of 4+ stars and 18 reviews.

Discount Book Man

Free to submit or pay $15 to upgrade to a featured listing.

eBooks Habit

Books must be $2.99 or less. It's free to submit, and they may or may not post it. For $10 you can get a guaranteed placement.

eBook Stage

Create an account and then you can submit your book for one of their promotions.

eReader Girl

It doesn't cost anything to submit your free book, but discounted or full price books are $20.

eReader Love

Free site to promote your book.

Free eBooks

Free books only.

Free Kindle Books 4U

Free to advertise, but they do not guarantee placement unless you donate to their site.

Free Today

Facebook page where you can post your book deal.

Frugal Freebies
Book must be free to promote here.

Gain Reads
For free or $0.99 books.

I Crave Freebies
Free books only.

Indies Today
Free to post your free book and $9 to post a sale book.

Inkitt
I've never tried Inkitt before, but they accept fiction submissions and advertise them on an app called Galatea. Click the link to their site for more information.

It's Write Now
For free and discounted books. $10 to guarantee your book will be promoted.

Korner Konnection
Fill out the form and your book will be promoted on their Facebook page.

New Free Kindle Books
Free to submit your free book, but they only promote 10% of submissions. For $5 you can get a guaranteed listing.

OHFB
Free to submit your book, but there's no guarantee that it will be selected.

Pretty Hot Books

On this site, you can choose the free version or upgrade for $25 to be listed on their front page for a week and for your book to be included in their newsletter.

Reading Deals

$29 for a guaranteed placement.

Topless Cowboy

This site promotes romance only, but you can submit romance suspense. You can upgrade to a feature listing for $20 and your book will be listed on their home page for five days, be included in their newsletter, and posted on social media.

CHEAP SITES TO PROMOTE ON

All Author

For $24 you can promote your books for six months.

Armadillo Ebooks

Free books only. $25 to promote your books on 15 different sites.

Author Shout

Prices start at $5 to advertise your book and go up from there.

Bargain Booksy (Written Word Media)

$60 to promote. Books must be between $0.99 and $5.00.

Book Barbarian

Books can ONLY be in the science fiction or fantasy genre, but I included them on this list because a supernatural suspense should be accepted. They only promote stand-alone novels or the first book in a series. Books must be free or at least 50% off regular price. 3.5 rating or higher. They are also booked out at least a month in advance. $25 to $55.

Book Bassett

Two options to promote here. Featured author post is $22 per day, and the cool thing is, you can submit up to five books to be promoted for that price. They also have a free book promotion deal for $9.

Book Doggy

$18 to $20. Your book is promoted on their site and in their newsletter.

Book Goodies

Prices start at $10. Free and discount books.

Book Gorilla

$50 to promote your free or $0.99 book and $100 to promote between the $1.00 and $2.99 price points.

Book Lemur

Free to $0.99 are $30

Book Raid

On this site, you pay per click, with a maximum charge of $40. Books must be discounted 50% or more and be at least 120 pages.

Book Reader Magazine

$20 to list your book on their site for a week.

BookSends

Price to advertise is between $50 and $100 depending on the discount of your eBook, which needs to be free to $2.99.

Books Loom

$15 to advertise your book.

Buck Books

Fiction books are $9 to promote. Your book must have a professional book cover, 10 favorable reviews, and be more than 60 pages long. They're interested in free or $0.99 books.

Budget Promotions

A budget book promo costs $18.

Digital Book Today

$20 to be the free featured book of the day.

eBook Deals Today

Book features for $5 to $10.

eBook Hounds

$50 to promote your book at any price point.

eReader IQ

$20-$40 to advertise, depending on sale price of the book. Books must be free or 50% off regular price. Books must have a minimum of 5 reviews and a good average.

eReader News Today

Books must be free or on sale, available on Amazon, full length, and professionally written and edited. Prices range between $50 and $120 depending on the discounted price of your book, which should be between free and $2.99.

Free & Discounted Books

This is for free books only. It's $12 if your book is free for a limited time and $35 if your book is permafree.

Free Books Hub

Three options here ranging in price from $10-$20.

Free Kindle Books & Tips

Prices start at $25 depending on the type of promo you want to run.

Genre Pulse

Free and $0.99 books. $18 to promote.

Good Kindles

Prices start at $25 to be listed on their homepage.

Hot Zippy

Prices start at $25.

Just Kindle Books

Prices start at $18 for a budget promotion.

Kindle Mojo

Prices start at $25.

Lovely Books

For $10 they'll promote your free book on over 40 Facebook groups.

Kindle Book Review

This is for free books with an average rating of 3.5 or higher. It's $20 to be the featured book of the day.

Many Books

$29 to be included in their newsletter.

My Book Place

$25 to have your book featured on their website for one week.

Pillow Talk Books

This is a site for romance promotions, but they accept romance suspense. It's $40 to advertise.

Planet Ebooks

Different pricing options depending on what you're after.

ReadFREE.ly

$10 to be featured in their newsletter. You can also pay a small fee to submit an author interview.

Real Romance Readers

$25 to have your email promoted on their mailing list. This site is romance only, but romance suspense should be accepted.

Robin Reads

For free or $0.99 books. Price ranges from $65 to $70 depending on book deal price. Book early on this site. They are easily booked out six weeks in advance.

Snicks List

You'll need to create an account on this site. Promotion starts at $5.

TCK Publishing

Books must have at least ten reviews, have a 4.0 star rating or higher, and be free or $0.99 on the sale date. $10 to advertise.

The eReader Café

There are a few different options here. It's $35 to be the featured book of the day, $30 to be the deal of the day, and $24 to be the daily spotlight.

The Fussy Librarian

Price depends on your book's genre. Books must be less than $5.99 and have a quality cover.

Unlimited Readers

Your book must be in Kindle Unlimited and remain there for at least thirty days. It's $9 to list your book in one genre and $15 to list in two.

White Dove Books

This site is for free kindle books. $20 to be promoted to their subscribers and their social channels.

Whizbuzz

$49 for a long-term promo that promotes your book on a specific day and over time.

SPENDY SITES TO PROMOTE ON

Author Ad Network

$129 to promote your book to 32 different sites. Some of them are sites not relevant to our genre though, so be sure to look the list of sites over before you make a purchase.

BookBub

Price depends on genre or subgenre and the price of your book, starting at $600 and up. The exposure is always worth it if you can get accepted.

Books Go Social
Prices between $89 and $499 depending on what you want them to do for you.

Freebooksy
$90 to feature your mystery.

Kindle Nation Daily
Variety of promo options. $30 to $130.

Riffle Books
Their main promo page states most genres are $150 to promote, but they will contact you for genre-specific pricing. Books must be free or at a 50% discount or more, professional, and at least 150 pages.

Other Ideas for Promoting Your Book

There are a lot of people who offer promotional services on Fiverr.

1. For $5, B KNIGHTS will promote your book to 4,800 readers on their site.

2. For $5, BOOK KITTY will promote your book on their Facebook pages, which has about 15k readers combined.

3. For $14, JAMES MAYFIELD will do a variety of promotions for your book, including posting it on Twitter, Reddit, and Pinterest.

4.   For $15, DTONG SPORTS will promote your book on his podcast.

5.   For $50, K LEVITT70 will create a one-minute commercial for your book, which will air on his podcast.

CHAPTER 35

LISTEN UP:
THE POWER OF AUDIOBOOKS

Audiobooks continue to get more popular as the years go on. And the great thing is, if you can't afford to pay for someone to produce your book, there are options where you can do a royalty share and still get your book recorded.

Audiobooks are a great way to make side money, and by maximizing the opportunities for your book to reach as many people as possible, you're not leaving money on the table.

Unless you're familiar with the recording process and have experience with it, I would not recommend trying to record a book yourself. I can always tell a narrator is new because the audio sounds like it was recorded in a tunnel. That's not the kind of first impression you want your listeners to have, and that is why you need to hire a professional.

Let's talk statistics.

There are several different options when it comes to what company to choose to publish your audiobook. My two favorites are ACX and Findaway Voices.

ACX

ACX brings together authors and narrators and provides a platform to distribute your books. You can narrate your own book, upload it to their site and use them to distribute it, or you can search for a narrator for your project and pay for production.

<u>Paying for production</u>

When you pay for production you pay a PFH rate (per finished hour). An estimate of the cost is generated when you enter the word count for your book, which is the average time it takes a narrator to read a book of that size.

You will distribute your book exclusively through Audible at a royalty rate of 40% or to be non-exclusive at a royalty rate of 25%. The exclusive 40% rate puts your book on Audible, Amazon, and iTunes. The 25% rate puts your book on those same sites and allows you to put the book on other sites as well.

<u>Royalty share and royalty share plus</u>

If you don't want to pay for production, your second option is to pay nothing up front and do a royalty split (share) with your narrator. You and your narrator will both receive a 20% royalty rate from the audio sales.

A third option is to choose Royalty Share Plus. This offers your narrator a one-time payment for the recording, plus they still receive 20% royalties from audio sales. This is a good option to choose if you don't want to pay a lot out of pocket for production, but you want a narrator who is more qualified than some of the others. Sometimes they're willing to do royalty share because they're new to recording and don't have many books under their belt. You can offer a stipend of $100 or $500 or whatever you're comfortable with to entice some of the more experienced narrators to audition for your project.

<u>How long is the Audible contract?</u>

The term is seven years, and once the term expires, it will automatically renew in one-year increments.

<u>What countries will the book be distributed?</u>

At the time of this writing: US, UK, Canada, France, Australia, and Japan

<u>Who sets the price?</u>

When you're publishing through ACX, they set the price, and it is determined by the length of the book. You'll also be paid different amounts depending on what type of download it is. They have a monthly subscription service for their listeners which still pays you per download, but it doesn't pay as much as someone who downloads it and isn't in the subscription service.

<u>If you're paying for production, how much should you pay PFH to your book's producer?</u>

I've found the more you're willing to spend, the more experienced your narrator will be. I tend to choose narrators in the $200 to $400 per hour range. It just depends on the book. Sometimes I'll offer $200 PFH to start, and if I don't find anyone I really like, I'll up the amount.

<u>What's the process? How does it work?</u>

Let's say you've just finished your book, and you're ready to search for a narrator/producer on ACX.

1. Log into your account and add your title.

2. Once it's added, you click on it and then choose how you want the audiobook produced (whether you're looking for a narrator or are going to upload your own recording).

3. Once you've chosen, you're taken to the ACX Book Posting Agreement page and that's where you'll want to read all the fine print to make sure you understand the terms and conditions of publishing your book. If you agree, select Agree and Continue.

4. Next you'll describe your book for your audience. I usually go with my book's blurb from its product page.

5. Enter the copyright information, which will be your name. The print copyright year is the year the book is being produced (the year we're in right now), and the audio copyright owner is also your name.

6. Select fiction for the type of book you've written and choose mystery and thrillers for the category.

7. Next you'll choose whether you want to start receiving auditions to find a narrator, or whether you know who you want to make an offer to already.

8. Now you need to decide what kind of narrator you're looking for. Do you want a male or a female? What age should they be? Should they have an accent? What vocal style should they have? I almost always choose storyteller as the vocal style because it suits my books well, but you'll want to choose whatever your vision is for your own books.

9. In the additional comments box, you want to sell yourself, especially if you're planning to do royalty share instead of PFH. Do not leave this blank if you're choosing the royalty share option. If you've ever won any awards, hit a bestseller list, or if your book has a great average ranking, put it all here.

The idea is to woo narrators in, because if they're recording your book for free, they want to know that there's a good chance it's going to sell and that they'll be able to recoup the time they invested when they receive their royalty checks. Another great thing to put here is how you plan to promote the book. What will you do to make sure people will download the book?

10. Next you'll upload your audition script. Keep it brief. No more than a couple of pages. Remember, they're auditioning for free without knowing whether you'll choose them or not. Their time is valuable, just like yours.

One other suggestion I'd like to make here is that you give them two different samples of approximately one page each or less. One sample should be narration (no dialogue between characters). This gives you an idea of the mood and tone of the narrator's voice and how it relates to the tone you feel is right for your story. For the second, take a snippet of dialogue between your main character and someone else. I like to choose dialogue between a man and a woman so I can hear how the narrator does with different voices.

11. On the next page, you can add in all the chapters of your book. This just helps streamline the process for the narrator.

12. Next you'll enter the word count of your book. A 60k book takes approximately 6.5 to record, so if you offer $200 PFH, for example, you'll end up paying around $1,300 for the entire production.

13. The territory is usually "World."

14. Select whether you want to be exclusive with Audible or have the freedom to distribute your book to other places.

15. Select whether you want to pay for the book's production or do royalty share. If you select royalty share, you'll be asked if you want to contribute to the production costs.

16. The last page is a summary of everything you've entered, so make sure to go over it for accuracy. ACX will also pull your average reviews from the book's product page and its current sales rank because these are things narrators will consider when they're deciding to choose your book or not.

I'd like to offer one last suggestion before moving on. When you narrow down your favorites from those who audition, I suggest you play their recordings for others to get their opinions as well. I narrow to three to five and then download the audios and have my Street Team vote on who they like the best and why.

Findaway Voices

The people behind Findaway Voices are nice and fabulous to work with from everything I know about them. I met with some of the team at a conference, and I was really impressed by what they had to say when it comes to creating a great alternative to ACX. They are very hands-on, which makes creating audiobooks with them as seamless as possible.

On their platform, your book will be distributed globally through retail, library, and education distribution channels (which is currently 45 different networks and growing).

Just like ACX, you also have the option to find a narrator or upload something you already have. If you're paying for production, narration costs start at $150 per hour and goes up to $550+.

<u>What makes Findaway stand out?</u>

A few differences between them and ACX is that they ask if your book is part of a series, and whether you want the same narrator for future books in the series. Another huge benefit is that you get to set your book's price. You also keep 80% of the royalty from every book sale. For example, let's say your book is priced at $10. The retailer takes $5, so you're left with a $5 royalty. Your share is $4 on that $10 book.

They also have an option called Voices Share, which means you can pay 50% of the production costs and then share 20% royalties with the narrator.

One other benefit is that Findaway has partnered with BookBub's Chirp audiobook promotional program.

CHAPTER 36

USA Today FOR THE WIN: HITTING A LIST

How does a book become a bestseller? And what tips can we learn from traditionally published books that we can try for ourselves?

In February of 2019, Alex Michaelides' first book *The Silent Patient* was published, and it immediately hit #1 on the *New York Times* bestseller list.

How did it make the list so fast after its debut?

You might be thinking, "It was backed by Macmillan Publishing, and they promoted the hell out of it."

And you'd be right. But they didn't just put it out and then throw money at it. A lot of planning was involved, and they started promoting the book an entire year before it was released.

Indie authors do things a lot differently. In a year's time, many of us will publish 2, 3, 4, 5+ books. Our advertising dollars are precious commodities. One of our goals is to find strategies that work for us, so we turn a profit without losing the farm in process.

An achievable list to strive for if you're trying to hit one is the *USA Today* Best-Selling Books list, so that's the one I'm going to focus on in this chapter.

Let's start off by talking about how many books you need to sell over a week (Monday through Sunday) to have a good chance at making the list. Unfortunately, the number fluctuates and there are always different variables at play.

If I'm trying to hit a list, my goal is to sell at least 7,000 books the week I want to make the list. Most of the time 7,000 gets me there, but not always. In the past, I've made the list with as little as 5,500 sales, and I've also missed the list on a book that had about 9,500 sales in a week (To this day, I'm still confused about what happened there).

Free books are not eligible to make the list, but paid books are, including books that are $0.99. In other words, as long as your book isn't free, you have a shot at making it, and the bigger the discount, the better your chances are. Eligible book formats include eBooks, paperback, and hardback, and it is possible to make the list with eBook sales alone.

The USA Today Best-Selling Books List collects data from many different book sales outlets, including bookstore chains, mass merchandisers, online bookstores, and independent bookstores, including:

- A.C. Vroman's Bookstore & Book Soup
- Amazon
- Apple Books
- Barnes & Noble
- Books-A-Million
- Costco
- Hudson Booksellers
- Joseph-Beth Booksellers
- Kobo

- Powell's Books
- R.J. Julia Booksellers
- Schuler Books & Music
- Target
- Tattered Cover Book Store

The top 150 top-selling titles are reported each week online, and 1-50 make the print version of the paper each week on Thursday for sales the previous Monday-Sunday.

The best strategy for making the list is to hit the ground running on Monday, so your sales start tallying right away and you have the entire week to keep the momentum going. Whenever possible I try to get a BookBub ad on a Monday. I can make the list without it, but BookBub ads give me my best chance for success. Whether I get a BookBub ad for the book or not, I promo stack every single day of the week by running at least three to four ads per day on different promo sites.

Once my daily promotions are in place, I plan out my ads. I rely heavily on Facebook ads, but I also create BookBub ads and Amazon ads as well. I test various ads a few weeks before I aim to make the list in order to determine which ads are the most successful. I then increase the ad spend on those ads.

On the first two to three days of the week, I like to get about 75% of the book sales I need to hit the list for the week. If I don't, I usually up the ad spend in an attempt to get the number where I want it to be.

Other things I sometimes do during push week:

- Send a newsletter to my subscribers telling them about the deal. I do this in two different ways:

1. The first is to send a newsletter to my entire list on a Tuesday, and then I send the same newsletter to anyone who didn't open the first one on Friday.

2. The second way is to divide my newsletter subscriber list by 5. Let's say I have 50k subscribers. I divide them by 5 and get 10k. I send the newsletter out in batches to 10k subscribers per day, over five days.

- Promote the sale on all social media and boost a post from my author page, targeting all those who follow the page.
- Do a newsletter swap with other authors, offering to promote one of their books on my newsletter that week if they promote mine in theirs. When I choose this option, I seek out some of my author friends who have at least 10k followers on their newsletter list.
- Ask/encourage my followers on social media and my Street Team to share the post I created about the book deal.

CHAPTER 37

COMING SOON:
BACK MATTER

The end of your book can be so much more than simply writing the words: THE END. It's valuable real estate that gives you the perfect opportunity to ask for sign-ups for your newsletter, to get the reader invested in the next book in the series, and to tell your readers about other books they may not have read yet.

<u>After my book ends, I write a personal message to the reader and say something like this:</u>

Thank you for reading *Little Girl Lost*, book one in the Georgiana Germaine mystery series.

I hope you enjoyed getting to know the characters in Gigi's world as much as I have enjoyed writing them for you. This is a continuing series with more books coming after the one you just read. You can find the series order (as of the date of this printing) in the "Books by Cheryl Bradshaw" section below. And if you're on Pinterest, be sure to check out Cheryl's photo inspiration for this series HERE.

In *Little Lost Secrets*, Book 2 in the series, Georgiana is swept up in a cold case murder when a dead body is found within the walls during a home renovation. How did the body get there? And what ties does it have to Georgiana's father's death more than three decades earlier?

Order *Little Lost Secrets* now by clicking HERE.

Want a sneak peek of *Little Lost Secrets*?

Here's an exclusive look at chapter one …

The first section in your back matter provides the reader with several different opportunities.

1. It links readers to an exclusive page where they can get a "behind the scenes" of the book while it's fresh in their minds.

2. It introduces the title to book two, the next book in the series.

3. It gives the reader a simple link to click and pre-order the next book.

4. It gives them a call to action by encouraging the reader to "Order by clicking here."

5. It gives the reader an exclusive sneak peek at the first chapter of the next book.

After the first chapter of the next book, there's another call to action so the reader doesn't have to backtrack in order to click on a link to purchase:

Enjoy the preview? Order *Little Lost Secrets* now by clicking HERE.

If you're writing a series, I highly recommend that you link one book to the next in this way. Even if you've just started writing the next book in the series, all you need to do is to have the first chapter written and edited in order to provide this for your readers.

Next, I invite the reader to join my newsletter list:

Never Miss One of Cheryl's Book's Again

Sign up for Cheryl Bradshaw's Killer Newsletter today to be one of the first to know when a new book is released. You'll also receive a FREE eBook for joining!
Sign up today by clicking HERE.

Next, I encourage them to leave a review:

You can show your appreciation for this book by leaving a review on Amazon, Barnes & Noble, Apple Books, Google Play, Kobo, or Goodreads. If you write a review, please be sure to email Cheryl HERE so she can express her gratitude. She does her best to reply to as many emails as she can, and she appreciates every piece of mail she receives.

…

I then give a brief bio:

About Cheryl Bradshaw

Cheryl Bradshaw is a *New York Times* and ten-time *USA Today* bestselling author writing in the genres of mystery, thriller, paranormal suspense, and romantic suspense, among others. Her novel *Stranger in Town* (Sloane Monroe series #4) was a 2013 Shamus Award finalist for Best PI Novel of the Year, and her novel *I Have a Secret* (Sloane Monroe series #3) was a 2013 eFestival of Words winner for Best Thriller.

All of Cheryl's books are heavily researched, proofed, and edited. Should you find any issues in the book you just read, please forward them to her assistant HERE so they can be sent along to the publisher.

...

And finally, I list my books in order and give a short introduction about what each one is about. I'll list the first two in my newest series below as a short example of what mine looks like.

Georgiana Germaine Series
Little Girl Lost (Book 1)
For the past two years, former detective Georgiana "Gigi" Germaine has been living off the grid, until today, when she hears some disturbing news that shakes her.

Little Lost Secrets (Book 2)
When bones are discovered inside the walls during a home renovation, Georgiana uncovers a secret that's linked to her father's untimely death thirty years earlier.

For each book, I make the title a hyperlink so readers can easily click and purchase.

And there you have it! The back matter I've just shown you is a good example to use in your own books, but I'd recommend doing a bit of homework and taking a look at the back matter of a dozen indie authors or so to get an idea of the kind of back matter you'd like to use in the back of your own books.

CHAPTER 38

BABY GOT BACK: BREATHING LIFE INTO YOUR BACKLIST

This chapter is for those of you who already have at least one series under your belt and want to know what you can do to bring it back to life if it's no longer selling well. It is my belief that a series book can sell forever if you're willing to make some adjustments.

1. Adjust the sales price

If you want to see an increase in sales, lowering the price for a certain amount of time isn't a bad idea. If your books are selling at $2.99, consider $0.99 or even free. If your books are $5.99, consider cutting the price in half and advertising the series at 50% off.

If you'd rather keep prices where they are, consider having the book at full price in the US, but discounted in other countries like Canada, Australia, and the UK. While I'm on the subject, do your prices in other countries end in $0.99? If they don't, consider changing them. Readers can easily become confused with strange pricing, like a book selling for $5.36.

2. Rewrite the first book in the series

I'm not saying to write a different book or to change what happens in book one. I am suggesting editing it again. Our writing style changes over time as we figure out our voice. Going back over the first book and making it better is always a good idea.

3. Revise the cover

I discussed this in a previous chapter, but I can't express how much difference a new cover can make. It can attract a whole new audience and give your book new life.

4. Rewrite the book description

How long has it been since you played around with your book description on your product page? I feel like I am always making little tweaks here and there, which usually happen because I've just read a book that gave me fresh ideas or because I've seen something on another author's page I thought was fantastic and wanted to see how something similar would work for me.

Speaking of reading books that help you, *Marketing Books on Amazon* by Rob Eagar is one I've just read, and he has a fantastic chapter on how to set up a successful product page.

5. Create a boxed set

If you haven't already, consider boxing all of your books in a series into one or two boxed sets. This is an easy way to publish a new book that you've already written, and to attract readers who are looking for a deal.

6. Write a prequel to the series

This is something I'm planning on doing for one of my series over the next few months. I'm excited about it because if I could go back in time, I would have written a different story for the first book. This gives me the chance to do that in a small way, and it can also entice readers if it's sold at a discount price.

Prequels don't need to be long. You can write a novella or even a novelette. The goal here is to write something that will get new readers involved in your series. I'd suggest selling something like this for $2.99 or less.

7. Run a promotion

I still run big ads for my backlist titles, and a lot of times, I spend more money advertising old books than new ones, especially if they're part of a series.

8. Work with a Co-Author

Co-authoring can be a great way to earn extra money and branch off into other subgenres if you work with the right person, someone who is motivated, has a similar vision to yours, and is committed to producing results in a timely manner. This year I've taken on a co-author to work with me on a spinoff of my main series. I am also considering working with other authors in the future.

CHAPTER 39

AND THE OSCAR GOES TO: AWARD SUBMISSIONS

For those of you who are interested in submitting your books for award consideration, I've put together a list of all the places authors can submit, and I have also included awards that are specific to the mystery/thriller/suspense genres. Some of the genre-specific awards are only open to authors who have been traditionally published, so be sure to check out each of them for their specific requirements.

<u>Agatha Awards</u> (Mystery)
The Agatha Awards honor mysteries that do not contain excessive gore or violence, explicit sex, and are not "hard-boiled." Eligible books are for the previous calendar year, and can be a hardback, paperback, or eBook. Ballots are sent via email in January of each year to all those who have registered for the Malice conference before the end of the previous year.

<u>Anthony Awards </u>(Mystery/Thriller)
The Anthony Awards are given each year at Bouchercon. The award got its name from Anthony Boucher, one of the founders of the Mystery Writers of America. Nominees and winners are selected by attendees.

<u>Arthur Ellis Awards</u> (Mystery/Thriller)
The Arthur Ellis Awards are Canadian literary awards and given by the Crime Writers of Canada. Awards are given for the best Canadian crime and mystery writing that were published the previous year. Recipients of the award must be Canadian citizens.

<u>Barry Awards</u> (Mystery/Thriller)
Named after Barry Gardner, and critic and lover of crime fiction, The Barry Awards are given at Bouchercon and are voted on by readers of the Deadly Pleasures mystery magazine.

Best Indie Book Award (Indie Award)
The "BIBA" Awards are given in multi genres in both fiction and nonfiction. Winners are also promoted in their newsletter and on social media.

<u>Bony Blithe Awards </u>(Mystery)
The Bony Blithe Award is awarded to Canadian citizens who have written "light" mysteries: cozy, satire, caper, humorous. Awards are presented each year at the Bony Blithe gala in Toronto.

<u>Dagger Awards</u> (Mystery/Thriller)
Dagger Awards are UK crime-writing awards. Most of the awards are nominated by publishers, with a few exceptions.

<u>Edgar Awards</u> (Mystery)
The Edgar Awards are presented by the Mystery Writers of America.

All works submitted must meet their requirements for Active Status membership, and they do not accept self-published work at this time.

Eric Hoffer Book Award (Indie Award)
This book award is given through the Eric Hoffer estate. A grand prize is given of $2,500 to one recipient each year.

Foreword Indies Book of the Year Award (Indie Award)
There are 56 categories of awards given by Foreword Reviews, and the top winners receive a $1,500 cash prize. Finalists are promoted through press releases, articles, and through social media.

Hillerman Prize (Mystery)
The Hillerman Prize is awarded to the best first mystery set in one of the Southwest states in the United States. I believe it is open to indie authors as well as traditionally published authors.

Independent Publisher Book Awards - IPPY (Indie Award)
The IPPY awards authors in over 100 categories, and award gold, silver, and bronze metals to the winners.

Indie Readers Discovery Award (Indie Award)
The Indie Readers Discovery Award started in 2010 and awards books of all genres in several different categories. There's a panel of judges who recommend the top winners.

Left Coast Crime "Lefty" Awards (Mystery/Thriller)
The Lefty Awards are chosen each year by members of the Left Coast Crime convention. Nominations are in January of each year in four different novel categories.

Macavity Awards (Mystery)
The Macavity Awards are voted upon members of the Mystery

Readers International. Awards are given in five different mystery categories.

Readers International. Awards are given in five different mystery categories.

National Indie Excellence Awards (Indie Award)
The National Indie Excellence Award is for paperback books only, not eBooks. They award books that demonstrate overall excellence through a synergy of form and content and are open to a variety of categories.

Ned Kelly Awards (Mystery/Thriller)
The Ned Kelly Awards are awarded by Australia's Crime Writers Association.

Nero Award (Mystery)
The "Nero" award is given by The Wolfe Pack for the best American Mystery for books written in the tradition of Rex Stout's Nero Wolfe series.

Next Generation Indie Book Awards (Indie Award)
Awards are given in over fifty categories by Next Generation, and finalists will be considered by a top agent for possible publication.

Readers Favorite Book Awards
The Readers Favorite Book Awards are given to indie, celebrity, and iconic authors.

Rubbery Book Prize (Indie Award)
The RBA Rubbery Book Award is an international based award open to indie authors from all countries. One grand award is given for the book of the year, and other awards are given in various genres. Winners will receive publishing consideration from a top London literary agency.

<u>Shamus Awards</u> (Mystery/Thriller)
The Shamus Awards are awarded by The Private Eye Writers of America each year. They must include a main character who is paid for investigative work, but not someone who is employed by the government, such as police officers, FBI agents, or detectives who work for the state department. It is open to indie authors.

<u>Thriller Awards</u> (Thriller)
The thriller awards are given out by ITW, the International Thriller Writers association. It is open to indie authors, but if you are not affiliated with a traditional publisher, you must pay dues in order to be eligible at this time.

<u>TopShelf Book Awards</u>
Established in 2020, the TopShelf Book Award is open to all indie, small press, and traditionally published authors. Cost is $100 per title for the first category, and $50 thereafter.

<u>Writer's Digest Self-Published Ebook Award</u> (Indie Award)
Winners of the Writer's Digest award receive a feature in the magazine and a paid trip to the conference. Ebooks must be between 40k and 100k to qualify.

CHAPTER 40

TURN IT UP: PUBLISHING 2.0

Successful indie authors know the best way to stay relevant in this business is to learn as much as you can and to keep your ear to the ground. Below is a list of several of my favorite sites that I believe are worth checking out.

Authors A.I.

Authors A.I. is a wonderful new resource where you can upload your manuscript and get an in-depth analysis of it in minutes. The Marlowe report is basically one-stop shopping for book analysis. It finds typos, tells you which words you've overused, finds cliches, gives you a dialogue vs. narrative breakdown, and so much more. I use it for every book I publish, and I am also one of their founding members and beta testers.

Book Candy Studios

Book Candy Studios make amazing book trailers for your books. I've always been impressed with the videos they create. They're among the best in the business.

Bookfunnel

BookFunnel is a great place to create attractive reader magnets for new subscribers who sign up for your newsletter. I also use them when I want to give away copies of one of my books or send ARCs to my readers.

Booksprout

Booksprout helps you build an ARC team using their team of readers and reviewers. They pair authors with readers interested in the books they like to read and alert those readers when you have a new book for them to read.

BookSweeps

BookSweeps is a great place to increase subscribers to your newsletter or to gain new BookBub followers. They run several giveaways each month in various genres. They have also introduced premium service options which allow you to have early access to upcoming promos, promotional discounts, ways to promote new releases and audiobooks, etc.

IngramSpark

IngramSpark allows self-published authors to distribute their books globally through their vast distribution networks.

k-lytics

This site gives you a lot of "inside" information on what's trending and happening in the market right now. It lists every category and sub-category in every genre. Using their system, you can find the best subgenre to write in right now and how to improve your book categories to maximize exposure.

MasterClass

MasterClass is a bit pricey, but if you can afford it, there are some great classes for writers in our genre, including: David Baldacci, James Patterson, Margaret Atwood, and Dan Brown. They've actually added a monthly billing option now too. One of my favorite things about their courses is that you can explore classes outside of the book genre as well, such as cooking and gardening. Once you subscribe, there's no limit on the number of classes you can take.

Pixie Publishing

After a decade of publishing both in the indie and traditionally published world, I've put together a talented team of editors, proofreaders, graphic designers, formatters, marketers, etc. and a handful of their services are now offered on Fiverr. Services include things like writing book descriptions, creating ad graphics, creating ad copy, and more, and we'll continue adding other services throughout the year. To learn more, look us up on Fiverr at cbradshaw.

Publisher Rocket

Dave Chesson of Kindlepreneur has come up with an amazing system that helps authors increase their book ranking on Amazon. Publisher Rocket (previously called KDP Rocket) helps you choose the right keywords for your books and ads and learn how to outrank your competitors.

Reedsy Discovery

With Reedsy Discovery you can upload your book before it's released or when it's just been released and gain exposure with readers in your genre. If the book piques the interest of one of the reviewers, you will also receive a review once they've read the book.

CHAPTER 41

KNOWLEDGE IS POWER: BOOK RECOMMENDATION LIST

I was watching Warren Buffet speak at a conference, and one piece of advice he gave to those looking to be successful is to "read, read, read." This same concept applies to us as authors. The more we read, the more we understand, and the more we understand, the more power we have to achieve success. On that note, I've put together a list of some of the best books I've read, some of which I've already mentioned throughout this book.

Ads

Ads for Author by Chris Fox

Amazon Ads for Authors by D M Potter

Amazon Ads Unleashed by Robert J. Ryan

BookBub Ads Expert by David Gaughran

Help! My Facebook Ads Suck by Mal Cooper & Jill Cooper

Mastering Amazon Ads by Brian D. Meeks

Author Success

2k to 10k by Rachel Aaron

5,000 Words Per Hour by Chris Fox

Advantage by Joe Solari

Become a Successful Indie Author by Craig Martelle

Book Launch by Chandler Bolt

How to Sell Books by the Truckload on Amazon by Penny C. Sansevieri

How to Write a Sizzling Synopsis by Bryan Cohen

Killing it on Kobo by Mark Leslie Lefebvre

Launch by Jeff Walker

Let's Get Digital by David Gaughran

Newsletter Ninja by Tammi Labrecque

Plot Gardening by Chris Fox

Pricing Strategies by Chris Martelle

Reader Magnets by Nick Stephenson

Release Strategies by Craig Martelle

Self-Editing for Fiction Writers by Renni Browne

Six Figure Author by Chris Fox

Supercharge Your Kindle Sales by Nick Stephenson

Take Off Your Pants by Libbie Hawker

Write Novels Fast by Shea Macleod

Write. Publish. Repeat. by Sean M. Platt and Johnny Truant

Marketing

Amazon Decoded by David Gaughran

Marketing Books on Amazon by Rob Eagar

Sell More Books with Less Marketing by Chris Syme

Write to Market by Chris Fox

Mystery/Thriller/Suspense Books

Don't Murder Your Mystery by Chris Roerden

Forensics by Val Macdermid

Forensics and Fiction, by D.P. Lyle

How to Write a Damn Good Mystery by James N. Frey

Howdunit Forensics, by D.P. Lyle

Howdunit Police Procedure & Investigation, by Lee Lofland

Howdunit, The Book of Poisons, by Serita Stevens

Murderous Minds by Dean A. Haycock

Stalling for Time by Gary Noesner

The Crime Book by DK and Cathy Scott

The Liar's Bible by Lawrence Block

The Liar's Companion by Lawrence Block

CHAPTER 42

WORDS OF WISDOM: ADVICE FROM TODAY'S BESTSELLING AUTHORS

As I was writing this book, I wrote to a handful of authors in the mystery/thriller genre. I asked them what advice they would give to a new author who was just starting out. Here is what they had to say:

This is my best advice: Curiosity is the first and finest tool of your trade.

Certainly you should spend time honing your craft, learning the ins and outs of the business, and studying the marketplace. But curiosity can be the fuel for all of that, nudging you to dig deeper and explore further, allowing you to mine ideas and build an ear for what will fascinate and compel a reader. More to the point, making the decision and the effort to become infinitely curious will serve your writing (particularly thriller writing) in ways you'll find both inconceivable and gratifying. Nurturing curiosity in yourself will give you an endless supply of grist for the mill—inspiration on demand, story starters that defeat the blank page, quipped turns of phrase and astounding historic facts that will delight and thrill and amaze your readers.

You can foster greater curiosity by simply embracing books, films, viewpoints, and ideas that might be outside of your current interests. Break your comfort zone and read a non-fiction book on a topic that bores you. Read novels with themes you aren't interested in. Watch films with subjects that you find bizarre. Listen to music that you've always ignored. And do it all with a mind open to growing. At times you may come away with nothing useful, but your newfound ability to seek inspiration anywhere and everywhere will become the sharpest, best tool in your belt. And any limitations you ever imagined you had will suddenly fall away. You'll be an uncommon writer, writing uncommon things.

Kevin Tumlinson is an award-winning and bestselling novelist, living in Texas and working in random coffee shops, cafés, and hotel lobbies worldwide. His debut thriller, The Coelho Medallion, *was a 2016 Shelf Notable Indie award winner.*

My advice to any author just starting out, is to ensure your work is up to scratch. By that, I mean, that you've employed an editor to cast their eye over it before you hit the publish button. If not, then your reviews are going to reflect your lack of effort. I've been in this business ten years now and I still use an editor and four proofreaders on each MS I write. To me, they're all a necessity. As authors, we're too close to our work to see the mistakes.

From the word go, I would also start building a newsletter, you will never know how important they are until a few years into your Indie career.

The next step, I would search Facebook for a couple of author groups where you can pick up fantastic information daily to help ease you into the tough journey ahead. I recommend 20Booksto50K and the SPF Community.

Finally, being an Indie author is a marathon not a sprint. As long as you're willing to put in the hours, a lot of hours, you will be a success.

M A Comley is a KINDLE UNLIMITED ALL-STAR author as well as being a New York Times, USA Today, Amazon Top 20 bestselling author, she has topped the book charts on iBooks as a top 5 bestselling and reached #2 bestselling author on Barnes and Noble with over two and a half million copies sold worldwide.

I have a close friend who lives in Ireland and spends his day writing novels. Once he's finished with one, he uploads it onto Amazon then moves on to the next. He probably sells a handful of books each year and never spends a minute trying to promote his work. I am very jealous. To him, this is success. I wish more of us could have his passion to write.

You see, if your goal is to be a *New York Times* bestseller, maybe you should rethink your objective. However, if you have this burning desire to have complete strangers smile and weep at the words you've written, then you're almost certain to attain your goal.

The most common advice given to writers is to just write. My advice is to write with passion. Write something you would want to read yourself. Be unique. Don't fit into a formula. Don't try to be the next James Patterson or Tess Gerritsen. Be the first you. And when you're done, should one person drop a solitary tear because of the words you've written. Congratulations, you're a successful writer.

__Author Gary Ponzo__ began his writing career thirty years ago by writing short stories. In just five years he'd published seven short stories in various publications, two of which were nominated for the very prestigious Pushcart Prize. His first novel, "A Touch of Deceit," won the 2009 Southwest Writers Novel Contest.

So—what advice would I give to a writer who is just starting out? Honestly, to investigate the business and learn how to do what you're trying to accomplish. There are many, many ways to be a writer. I was a practicing lawyer for years. For me, lawyering was writing -- with a better paycheck.

Many writers write for the love of it and never try to publish. Many more write as a hobby, keeping the day job. Some writers pursue a traditional publishing career, and others decide to start their own writing business. What do you want to do? The clearer your vision for your writing life, the more likely you are to achieve it and be satisfied with it.

When I started writing fiction, I had no idea how little money most fiction writers made. I also had no idea how long the road to publication would be. These days, there's a lot of information out there to help you determine what you want -- and how to get it. I'd encourage you to take advantage of that and follow your dreams.

Award-winning New York Times, USA Today and #1 Amazon Bestselling Author **Diane Capri's** *work is "Full of thrills and tension, but smart and human, too," says #1 worldwide publishing phenomenon Lee Child. Diane is the past Executive Vice President of International Thriller Writers, past member of the Board of the Florida Chapter of Mystery Writers of America, and active in Sisters in Crime and other writing organizations.*

First: If you have the passion to write—and not just idle fantasies about "being a writer"—then *you must write*, every single day. All successful professional writers block out daily writing time. They keep that work period sacred, allowing no interruptions or distractions—from family, pets, phone calls, doorbells, and especially email and social media. So, shut the door, shut off your web browser, sit at your writing spot, set an output goal for the day's session—then meet that quota before you leave. If you do that, manuscript pages will pile up fast, and you'll have a book—and a writing career—before you know it.

Second: *Honor your craft.* I know many writers with creative imaginations, but inspiration alone is not enough to build a successful career. You are competing with the finest authors in the world for reader eyeballs and loyalty. So, you must study, practice, and master the basics of the writing craft. Besides reading books and attending seminars, study closely the works of writers you respect. See how they develop plot structure and pacing, characterization and dialogue.

Third and finally: *Be patient.* Don't expect success—however you personally define it—with your early work. Almost all bestselling authors had to write many manuscripts before eventually finding their voice and their audience. But if you truly have the passion to write, and the discipline to write constantly and hone your craft, your readers *will* eventually find you.

__Robert Bidinotto__ is the author of the #1 Kindle bestselling thriller, "HUNTER," its award-winning sequel, "BAD DEEDS," and the newly released "WINNER TAKES ALL." He's also been a widely published, award-winning investigative journalist, magazine editor, and nonfiction author.

A lot of people are going to give you a lot of advice about everything from how to write a great book to how to market that book. Not all that advice is good. Not all that advice will work for you. But, in my opinion, the worst writing advice ever given is this: Write what you know.

Nonsense.

Yeah, yeah, I know the guy who said it is ridiculously famous, but not even he took his own advice. I write cozy mysteries rife with murders, and I've never killed anybody. I haven't solved any mysteries either, now I think about it. Frankly, if everyone wrote only what they knew, there would be no science fiction, no fantasy, no vampires (sparkly or otherwise). How boring life would be! Instead, I say, write what you love. Write what you're passionate about. Write what excites you, scares you, thrills you. Pour your heart and soul into it and all that joy will come out on the page. It can't help it. Anything you need to know can be discovered as you go. That, dear author, is what research is for.

***Shéa MacLeod** is the author of urban fantasy, post-apocalyptic, sci-fi, contemporary, and paranormal romances, and cozy mysteries. She's an international bestseller of the Sunwalker Saga series as well as the post-apocalyptic series Dragon Wars, the Cupcake Goddess novelettes, and the action-packed sci-fi romance series, Omicron ZX. She's also written contemporary romance romcom, Notting Hill Diaries. She is currently working on her two cozy mystery series, Viola Roberts Cozy Mysteries and Lady Rample Mysteries, as well as Wolffe & Bane, a new paranormal mystery series co-written with Miranda Mayer.*

My advice to any author starting out is simple but incredibly difficult to achieve: develop a really thick skin. You're going to be as devoted to your work as you are to your children or your significant other, and it's going to feel like every person along the way in the publishing process is intent on picking it apart. From your agent, to your editor, to your publisher, to your readers, everyone will seem to delight in pointing out the wart on your baby's nose. Your job will be to separate the wheat from the chaff within all that criticism, while putting aside your own feelings of defensiveness. If you can do that effectively, your baby will become even more beautiful than you ever imagined. You might even earn a few loyal readers along the way.

***Allan Leverone** is the New York Times and USA Today bestselling author of twenty-two novels and five novellas, and a former winner of the prestigious Derringer Award for excellence in short mystery fiction. His chilling novel, MR. MIDNIGHT, was included in Suspense Magazine's "Best Books of 2013" issue.*

What's this I hear—you want to be a writer? Good for you. Regardless of the format you've chosen, there's nothing more important than self-expression. And the precious gift of communicating your thoughts and ideas in written words . . . it's more than important, it's downright honorable.

Fledgling novelists often ask me for advice on the process of writing, and though I shy away from lecturing, here's a tip you might find helpful.

JUST WRITE—Let your ideas flow and memorialize them. Don't worry about being good and don't worry about being judged. The more you write the better you'll become. You may get published or you may not. You might sell a million copies of your work or just a few. Get it into your head right now—no one's opinion of your work is more important than your own. Agents and editors may be the gatekeepers of the literary world but they're not the arbiters of quality work.

Write every day, write passionately, and enjoy the process. As Emerson said, "It's not the destination, it's the journey."

***Lawrence Kelter** never expected to be a writer. In fact, he was voted the student least likely to step foot in a library. Well, times change,* *and he has now authored several novels including the internationally bestselling Stephanie Chalice and Chloe Mather Thriller Series, as well as the new adventures of My Cousin Vinny. Early in his writing career, he received support from literary icon Nelson DeMille, who was gracious enough to put pencil to paper to assist in the editing of the first book, and felt strongly enough about the finished product to say, "Lawrence Kelter is an exciting new novelist, who reminds me of an early Robert Ludlum."*

The most important thing you can do as an author starting out is to know what your goal is. That understanding drives everything else you do. Are you going to do it just for catharsis, the old "I just wanted to write a book" reason, or do you want to be a writer for a living? One will lead you down a path of market research and investigation, learning about what works and what doesn't for authors in your genre.

You'll also need to learn a litany of marketing skills if you want to give yourself a real chance at making a living as a writer. If you just want to write a book to see if you can, or to simply put your idea into the universe, none of those things really apply. If you want to be a professional writer, you must pull back the veil and learn how all the gears work for successful authors.

On the writing side of things, learning your true voice is the second most important thing behind knowing your goal. It takes some authors several books before they figure out their true storytelling voice. It took me at least five, not including the short stories. One thing that helps with this discovery is reading. Read books in your genre first. As you begin to hone your skills and tighten the way you tell stories, you can expand out into other genres and incorporate certain skills and word usage into your own flow, making them your own, and bringing a new layer of storytelling to your readers.

The third, and absolutely critical thing new writers need to do is be persistent and consistent. It's easy to see success stories of Writer A who published three books in three months with no audience and went from zero to 30k a month in 90 days and think that's easily repeatable. It's also easy to see Writer B who published a smash hit with book one and continued crushing it through book 4 and think that all you have to use is his or her methods.

Every author is different. Every journey is different. Yours will not look like anyone else's. It might be book three that sets the world on fire or it could be book twenty. But if you write consistently every day, five days a week, and you persist in publishing new work multiple times a year, you are taking care of multiple pieces of the puzzle at one time.

As you write, you will learn your voice. You will also build your catalog, which will get you closer to your ultimate goal of being a professional writer. Remember, don't compare yourself to others. Don't fall prey to wondering why it took someone only three books to hit their goal while you've written eleven and it's still slogging along. Maybe you need to switch to a new series, a new character, a new genre. It happens.

That leads to another piece of advice. You should write what you love to read or watch. I love Indiana Jones, Goonies, National Treasure, Scooby Doo, and books of that ilk. I'm not out there trying to write urban fantasy, even though I think it's cool. I write what I love and understand. I grasp the concept of story flow for my genre. Don't try to swim upstream.

Lastly, the most important advice I can offer is giving. Give freely to the world, to your readers. Not just a free novella or short story or even a full novel. Those things are great, and they can get you new readers, but keep giving. Give them sneak peek chapters. Give them cover reveals. Make them a part of the universe you've created. Share pictures of you in cool places, even if it's just your balcony. Share stories with them via video on YouTube or social media. Write a new short story you give them just for the fun of it. Give a portion of your royalties to charity and give your time to other authors who are looking for help. That's my advice to new authors. Heed these principles, and you will have set the pieces in place for long term, sustained success.

Ernest Dempsey *is the USA Today bestselling author of the Sean Wyatt adventure series and has written over forty novels to date. His archaeological thrillers have been enjoyed by millions of people all over the world.*

The only aspiring writer is a writer who is not writing. If you're writing—whether every day, once a week or once a month—you are a writer, not an aspiring one. And writer's write. We put our butts in a chair and put something on paper (real or virtual) as often as we can.

If you don't have a lot of time, start small. Write a paragraph on the book idea you've been thinking about. Write a sentence for a story you may never finish. Or just write a grocery list with a little flare. Eventually, without you even realizing it, you'll find more time here and there, and that sentence will become a paragraph, and that paragraph a page, and that page a chapter.

I was an aspiring writer for years. When I finally told myself it was now or never, I started getting up an hour early, and writing before getting ready for work. I wrote three novels this way, in four years, one of which brded up being my first published novel.

Maybe getting up early isn't an option for you. What about taking fifteen minutes at lunch to jot something down? Or thirty after everyone else goes to sleep to flesh out a character? If it's just not possible to do that now, that's okay. A point will come when the time will be there. Just be sure to recognize it when it arrives.

Brett Battles *is a* USA Today *bestselling and Barry Award-winning author of over thirty-five novels, including the Jonathan Quinn series and its Excoms spinoff, the Project Eden series, and the time bending Rewinder series. He's also the coauthor, with Robert Gregory Browne, of the Alexandra Poe series. He is one of the founding members of Killer Year and is a member of Mystery Writers of America and International Thriller Writers.*

New Writers Should Read a Lot

In their genre, that is. If you're going to write action/thrillers or hard-boiled mystery, read and watch a whole lot of action/thrillers and hard-boiled mystery. Forget the crap they make you read these days in the English classes in high school. Chances are they choose books that are "woke" and "inclusive" and, even if they're good, it's not the stuff you should be reading. Unless you want to, that is. Read what you love, and one day you will love what you write.

New Writers Should Write a Lot

That means ass in the chair time. What did some genius surmise about mastering one's art? You need 10,000 hours of practice until you can perfect your craft. That's of course, a bunch of BS, but it sounds good. But the fact remains, writing is like a muscle. You either use it or lose it. You need to write every day, no matter what comes your way. COVID-19, war, famine, divorce(s), sick kids, piles of bills that haven't been paid, Christmas, your birthday, whatever. Like Picasso said to his buddy when said buddy asked him why he never spent more time with his kids. "Because I never would have accomplished anything," Picasso responded.

New Writers Shouldn't Chase Trends

I'm partially guilty of this by doing things like putting "Girl" in one of my titles, The Girl Who Wasn't There. But that's as far as I go. If you're already telling yourself you're going to write the next Harry Potter, well, that ship has sailed, my friend. Remember the vampire bandwagon? And chick lit? I just kept on writing what I loved to read, which in my case is hard-boiled crime, noir, and psychological suspense, among other genres. This keeps me writing every day and enjoying my job. If you chase trends, chances are, by the time you've finished your book, the trend will have passed. That's why they're called trends.

New Writers Should Publish Independently and Traditionally

The old ways of publishing are dying not a slow death, but because of this horrid pandemic (this is being written in December of 2020), a rapid death. I predict that within a couple of years, the majority of major authors will be selling directly to their audience rather than going through a publisher. Or, like me, they will do both (I put out so much material there's no way a single publisher could handle it all, unless they want to pay me millions, which they don't). Speaking of advances: since there are currently only 4 big publishers left, advances will be getting smaller and smaller and smaller. I started out with a quarter million-dollar advance from Delacorte in '99. I've had a bunch of nice and very nice advances since then, but nothing that big. Small advances are the wave of the future, which means, look forward to creating multiple streams of writing income.

So, there you have it. Some advice for the new writer. It's not everything you need to know. But it's food for thought from a 25-year veteran of the professional writing and publishing wars. Take it or flush it. It's up to you. But one thing is for sure, once again, the times are changing, and changing fast.

Vincent Zandri is the New York Times *and* USA Today *bestselling ITW Thriller Award and PWA Shamus Award winning author of more than 40 novels and novellas including* The Girl Who Wasn't There, The Remains, *and the Dick Moonlight, PI series. He was also a finalist for the 2019 Derringer Award for Best Novelette.*

Being a good author requires a deep commitment to the craft. With literally thousands of new books being published each week and new authors cropping up all the time, you have to have a good idea about what you want to do with your writing. And if you want to be a full-time author, you must make a heavy investment on plying your skill and getting better at it each time.

Nathaniel Hawthorne once wrote, "An author's last work is always his best one, in his own estimate, until it quite loses the red heat of composition. After that, it falls into its true place, quietly enough."

What's important to understand about that quote is that you should always feel like you're improving in one way or another by virtue of being intentional about improving. Sometimes, I focus more on making my dialogue crisper. Other projects, I might make it a point to weave in more complexities into my plot. Or perhaps I want to create more depth in the relationship between the two main characters. But whatever facet I'm focusing on, I want to think it's better than the last one I wrote. But like Hawthorne notes, eventually it falls into a pecking order among your works.

Now, get out there and write so eventually you have a difficult time determining just how good your latest work really is in light of all the others you pen.

R.J. Patterson is an award-winning writer and thriller author living in the Pacific Northwest. While growing up in a military family, he spent some of his formative years living with his family on the estate of an English baron and baroness. It was there that he developed his passion for good literature and an appreciation for football. Upon returning to the United States, R.J. entered the field of journalism where he won numerous writing awards and has written articles for many prestigious U.S. newspapers, including the New York Times.

READ. We all need inspiration and models. Read what you love and find successful writers in that genre. You don't want to copy them, but you want to observe how they achieve the results that you love. This can become an aim for your own writing. READ BOOKS ON WRITING. There are some great instructional books out there with practical advice on bringing your writing to a high level. Be sure to read: STEIN ON WRITING by Sol Stein, STORY by Robert McKee, SELF-EDITING FOR FICTION WRITERS by Renni Browne, and Dave King DARE TO BE BAD. This was the best advice given by my first writing mentor Dean Wesley Smith.

We are our own worst critics and we let that inner critic cause us to stall. One of the most important things a writer can do is to overcome their fear of writing badly. Often, our writing isn't nearly as bad as we think. It's not always great, but guess what? It can only get better if you do one thing: WRITE. So, dare to write badly, give yourself permission. Even if it is bad, it's just a first draft. You can improve it and that process makes you a better writer. There is only one way to improve a blank page: WRITE!

Joshua Graham *is the* New York Times *and* USA Today *bestselling author of* Beyond Justice, Terminus, *and* Darkroom, *the winner of the International Book Award, Forward National Literature Award, USA Book News Best Books Award, and host of Thriller Radio.*

1. Commit to your writing. If it's not a drive inside you, a kind of hunger, do something else with your life. While writing can be fun at times, it requires a lot of time and energy and it'll mean stepping away from things you could be doing instead.

2. Decide where you want to be in five years and figure out how much work you'll need to do to get there. (Although my theory is if you want to completely change your life it can be done within two years, with a lot of work and effort.)

3. Commit to the genre you love writing in, no matter what genre, but be wise enough to love a genre that people generally want to read.

4. Read in every genre if a book piques your curiosity even slightly. You'll start reading less for pleasure and more to see how different writers do things, which is one of the not-great side effects

of writing for a living. You'll begin to see frameworks and character arcs with many novels. You may marvel at a writer's abilities, but it puts you in a different chair than when you read for pleasure and escape only. Your innocence as a reader will be gone.

5. Read the biographies of writers throughout time. Our lives tend not to be too much different from each other in terms of the work. Anthony Trollope's journal of how he'd get up early before his regular job and write a specific amount to produce a huge body of work is inspiring.

6. "Starting out" depends on your age. I began seriously determining I'd be a novelist from age 5 on, typing stories on an old typewriter by age 8. I never veered from writing all that time. Yet I didn't write my first novel until I was 27 because it took that long for me to believe I could produce something worth being published. I had written novellas prior to this but never felt they were good enough; and I was right.

7. If you really want to do this, do the research on aspects of the business. Read the books out there, Google articles and interviews with people who might know. Do not just email established writers and ask for all their wisdom and knowledge. They have work and lives and there's a lot of good information in books and online. Books like the one you've just read.

8. Walk the walk. Do the thing you're supposed to be doing: write the book, And then the next one. Keep studying what makes a story, whether in film, a dinner conversation, a joke, or a book.

9. Don't ask why something was published when it's not to your taste, ask what does that story do that got people interested? How did that writer manage to create something people want to read?

10. Never stop learning.

11. Got self-doubt? Laugh at it. Lack confidence? Confidence is a mask. You take it on and off, but the genuine state of a writing is that the story is more important than how you feel that day or that week. It needs to live, and it doesn't care if you believe in yourself or not, it just wants to come alive. Serve the story. Do the work.

12. Bring your stories to life. Your wit, your intelligence, your technical skills, your knowledge of language, your experience of emotions and psychological states, your understandings of how things work, of people and places—all of it will play into the story. And if there's something you don't know that you need to know, learn about it.

13. Finally, you get to make up your own adventure as a writer. Where do you want to submit? To NY publishers? Or self-publish? Or get an agent now? Or never use an agent? It is up to you and no one else can make these decisions for you. I've done all of that and I know from 30 years of experience there is no "one way only" to have a successful writing career. Just create the stories and figure out what you and you alone want to do with them. Then study, search on the internet for information, and follow-through on what it is you want from your writing career.

None of this is asking a lot of you once you've committed to writing for a living.

Douglas Clegg is a writer of imaginative dark fiction (including horror, gothic, fantasy, supernatural, and suspense thrillers) and has been a professional novelist since he signed his first book contact with Simon & Schuster in 1987. His books have been published worldwide and translated into various editions. His short fiction has won the Bram

Stoker Award, the International Horror Guild Award, and the Shocker Award, and has been included in several Years' best anthologies.

THANK YOU!

Thank you for reading this book. It is my sincerest hope that it helped/benefitted you in some way. If there was a topic you were hoping to learn about that you didn't see, please let me know. I'm open to doing a 2.0 version to fill in any gaps I may have left out. Please take a moment to leave a review. It would be much appreciated!

BOOKS BY CHERYL BRADSHAW

Sloane Monroe Series

Black Diamond Death (Book 1)
Charlotte Halliwell has a secret. But before revealing it to her sister, she's found dead.

Murder in Mind (Book 2)
A woman is found murdered, the serial killer's trademark "S" carved into her wrist.

I Have a Secret (Book 3)
Doug Ward has been running from his past for twenty years. But after his fourth whisky of the night, he doesn't want to keep quiet, not anymore.

Stranger in Town (Book 4)
A frantic mother runs down the aisles, searching for her missing daughter. But little Olivia is already gone.

Bed of Bones (Book 5) (*USA Today* Bestselling Book)
Sometimes even the deepest, darkest secrets find their way to the surface.
Flirting with Danger (Book 5.5) A Sloane Monroe Short Story
A fancy hotel. A weekend getaway. For Sloane Monroe, rest has finally arrived, until the lights go out, a woman screams, and Sloane's nightmare begins.

Hush Now Baby (Book 6) (*USA Today* Bestselling Book)
Serena Westwood tiptoes to her baby's crib and looks inside, startled to find her newborn son is gone.

Dead of Night (Book 6.5) A Sloane Monroe Short Story
After her mother-in-law is fatally stabbed, Wren is seen fleeing with the bloody knife. Is Wren the killer, or is a dark, scandalous family secret to blame?

Gone Daddy Gone (Book 7) (*USA Today* Bestselling Book)
A man lurks behind Shelby in the park. Who is he? And why does he have a gun?

Smoke & Mirrors (Book 8) (*USA Today* Bestselling Book)
Grace Ashby wakes to the sound of a horrifying scream. She races down the hallway, finding her mother's lifeless body on the floor in a pool of blood. Her mother's boyfriend Hugh is hunched over her, but is Hugh really her mother's killer?

Sloane Monroe Stories: Deadly Sins

Deadly Sins: Sloth (Book 1)
Darryl has been shot, and a mysterious woman is sprawled out on the floor in his hallway. She's dead too. Who is she? And why have they both been murdered?

Deadly Sins: Wrath (Book 2)

Headlights flash through Maddie's car's back windshield, someone following close behind. When her car careens into a nearby tree, the chase comes to an end. But for Maddie, the end is just the beginning.

Deadly Sins: Lust (Book 3)

Marissa Calhoun sits alone on a beach-like swimming hole nestled on Australia's foreshore. Tonight, the lagoon is hers and hers alone. Or is it?

Deadly Sins: Greed (Book 4)

It was just another day for mob boss Giovanni Luciana until he took his car for a drive.

Deadly Sins: Envy (Book 5)

A cryptic message. A missing niece. And only twenty-four hours to pay.

Georgiana Germaine Series

Little Girl Lost (Book 1)

For the past two years, former detective Georgiana "Gigi" Germaine has been living off the grid, until today, when she hears some disturbing news that shakes her.

Little Lost Secrets (Book 2)

When bones are discovered inside the walls during a home renovation, Georgiana uncovers a secret that's linked to her father's untimely death thirty years earlier.

Little Broken Things (Book 3)

Twenty-year-old Olivia Spencer sits at her desk in her mother's bookshop, dreaming about her upcoming wedding. The store may be closed, but she's not alone, and her dream is about to become her worst nightmare.

Addison Lockhart Series

Grayson Manor Haunting (Book 1)
When Addison Lockhart inherits Grayson Manor after her mother's untimely death, she unlocks a secret that's been kept hidden for over fifty years.

Rosecliff Manor Haunting (Book 2)
Addison Lockhart jolts awake. The dream had seemed so real. Eleven-year-old twins Vivian and Grace were so full of life, but they couldn't be. They've been dead for over forty years.

Blackthorn Manor Haunting (Book 3)
Addison Lockhart leans over the manor's window, gasping when she feels a hand on her back. She grabs the windowsill to brace herself, but it's too late--she's already falling.

Belle Manor Haunting (Book 4)
A vehicle barrels through the stop sign, slamming into the car Addison Lockhart is inside before fleeing the scene. Who is the driver of the other car? And what secrets within the walls of Belle Manor will provide the answer?

Till Death do us Part Novella Series

Whispers of Murder (Book 1)
It was Isabelle Donnelly's wedding day, a moment in time that should have been the happiest in her life...until it ended in murder.

Echoes of Murder (Book 2)

When two women are found dead at the same wedding, medical examiner Reagan Davenport will stop at nothing to discover the identity of the killer.

Stand-Alone Novels

Eye for Revenge (*USA Today* Bestselling Book)

Quinn Montgomery wakes to find herself in the hospital. Her childhood best friend Evie is dead, and Evie's four-year-old son witnessed it all. Traumatized over what he saw, he hasn't spoken.

The Perfect Lie

When true-crime writer Alexandria Weston is found murdered on the last stop of her book tour, fellow writer Joss Jax steps in to investigate.
Hickory Dickory Dead (USA Today Bestselling Book)
Maisie Fezziwig wakes to a harrowing scream outside. Curious, she walks outside to investigate, and Maisie stumbles on a grisly murder that will change her life forever.

Roadkill (*USA Today* Bestselling Book)

Suburban housewife Juliette Granger has been living a secret life ... a life that's about to turn deadly for everyone she loves.